CAN WE TEACH CHILDREN TO BE GOOD?

Can We Teach Children To Be Good?

Basic issues in moral, personal and social education

New Edition

Roger Straughan

Open University Press
Milton Keynes · Philadelphia

Open University Press
Open University Educational Enterprises Limited
12 Cofferidge Close
Stony Stratford
Milton Keynes MK11 1BY
and
242 Cherry Street, Philadelphia, PA 19106, USA

First Published 1982 by Allen and Unwin
This new edition first published 1988
Copyright this edition © Roger Straughan 1988

British Library Cataloguing in Publication Data
Straughan, Roger, *1941–*
    Can we teach children to be good? : basic
    issues in moral, personal and social
    education. – New ed.
    1. Schools. Moral education – Philosophical
    perspectives
    I. Title
    370.11'4

    ISBN 0-335-09525-9
    ISBN 0-335-09524-0 Pbk

Library of Congress Cataloguing-in-Publication Data
Straughan, Roger.
    Can we teach children to be good? : basic issues in moral, personal, and
social education/Roger Straughan.--New ed.
        p.   cm.
    Bibliography: p.
    Includes index.
    ISBN 0-335-09524-0 (pbk.)   ISBN 0-335-09525-9
    1. Moral education. 2. Education--Philosophy. 3. Education--Aims
and objectives. I. Title.
LC268.S8 1988
370.11'4--dc19   88-19688 CIP

Printed in Great Britain

For Eleanor – who hopes that we can't.

Contents

Foreword to New Edition

Since the first edition of this book appeared in 1982, there has been a number of significant developments within the area of moral education. A steady stream of books has been published, dealing with both theoretical and practical aspects of the subject; these are referred to, where appropriate, in this new edition. More specifically, increased interest has been shown in methodological and curricular questions concerning classroom practice, and this has tended to be associated with a linguistic, conceptual shift away from 'moral' and towards 'personal and social' education.

These trends call for careful scrutiny and analysis, for it is always dangerous to assume that any educational change is necessarily for the better. Consequently, more attention is paid in this edition both to the range of practical approaches which have developed in recent years and to the issue of 'personal and social education'.

The main emphasis and concern of the book, however, remain unashamedly unaltered. These recent trends indeed make it even more imperative that we continue persistently to address the basic question of what exactly we are trying to achieve in this area, and this will never be satisfactorily answered by concentrating exclusively upon methodological matters or by tinkering with terminology. Plato would probably still see the subject of moral education today to be 'in utter confusion', and we still cannot afford to ignore the logic of his proposed strategy for clearing it up.

R.S.

For my part, Protagoras, when I see the subject in such utter confusion I feel the liveliest desire to clear it up. I should like to follow up our present talk with a determined attack on virtue itself and its essential nature. Then we could return to the question whether or not it can be taught...

Plato, Protagoras, 361C

1: What Are the Problems?

Most people, if asked what the main job of teachers is, would probably give an answer like 'To pass on knowledge', or 'To develop children's intellectual abilities', or 'To prepare youngsters for future employment'. At times like the present, therefore, when there are allegations of falling educational standards, teachers are likely to be blamed for failing to deliver these particular goods: children, it may be argued, do not know as much as they should, or do not know the right things, or are failing to achieve certain basic levels of skill and competence, or are ill-equipped to earn a living when they leave school.

But these are not the only grounds on which charges are made, rightly or wrongly, about falling standards in schools, and teachers are criticized for not doing their job properly. For many people, talk of falling standards brings to mind standards of *behaviour* and *conduct* rather than of intellectual attainment, and to judge from such hallowed barometers of public opinion as *Any Answers* or radio 'phone-in' programmes teachers are to be held largely responsible for this kind of decline also; they should teach children not only to be knowledgeable, but also to be good.

Let us try to spell out in more detail the precise failure of duty of which teachers are here being accused. The argument usually goes something like this. Modern society is becoming increasingly more lawless, violent, undisciplined and permissive, and this trend is most apparent among the younger generation. Statistics show that vandalism, violent crime, drug-taking and sexual activity have risen and are rising among teenagers. Less sensational but equally significant, it is claimed, is a general decline in such things as respect for authority, politeness and good manners, resulting in children today being ruder, using more bad language and caring less about their appearance and dress than ever before. Schools must be held in part to blame for this state of affairs, for it is their products which are failing to come up to the desired standard. Teachers are not doing enough to impart the right values to children, and to ensure that their behaviour is socially acceptable.

Decreasing interest in religion generally, and in religious education in particular, is often picked out in this kind of argument as an important contributory factor to our alleged moral malaise. Christian teaching used to provide clear answers to questions about right and wrong, and left children in no doubt about these answers. Nowadays, not only has the number of church-going parents steadily fallen, but the emphasis upon religion in schools has also diminished, it is claimed, to the point where in practice it is often difficult to detect anything that could count as 'religious' in many schools. So, the argument goes, a moral vacuum has been created in the classroom, and consequently it is even more vital that teachers should now make plain to pupils of all ages what is the right way to behave both in and out of school. Indeed, in view of the virtual eclipse of religion in schools, should not a place now be allocated on the timetable to 'moral education'?

Let us rather grandly label this set of claims and opinions 'the moralistic argument'. We hear versions of it voiced quite frequently in many quarters, and it tends to gain support and approval from a wide variety of people because it somehow 'sounds right'. Surely standards of behaviour among the young *have* fallen, and schools *have* therefore opted out of providing a clear moral lead; not enough time and attention are being devoted to the business of teaching children to be good.

But arguments which 'sound right', and which may have a strong emotional appeal for many people, should not be swallowed whole. Before any such set of views is accepted, it must be subjected to critical scrutiny and probing, especially if, as in this case, its implications are so serious. If we do decide that this argument is valid, we are agreeing that a particular, undesirable state of affairs exists among children, that that state of affairs can be remedied, and that teachers are failing in their moral, social and educational obligations by not remedying it. It is especially important for those preparing to become teachers to have worked out where they stand on these issues, as this will radically affect their attitude towards teaching, and will help to determine what sort of teachers they will become. A strong sense of missionary zeal and a vocational commitment towards reforming the young, for example, would be the likely characteristics of entrants to the teaching profession who assented to this 'moralistic argument'. If, then, a teacher's response to the question of whether we can and should teach children to be good is going to have a direct and practical pay-off, in terms of how he actually sees his job and behaves in the classroom, it is essential that he at some time gives that question careful, rational consideration, and does not base his classroom practice merely upon unexamined assumptions about his teaching role.

How can we ensure that these assumptions do not go unexamined? One way is to try to do some *philosophical* thinking about the basic issues, for it is one of the main functions of philosophy to do just that – to take our existing intuitions and beliefs, and expose them to a particular kind of testing. The tests that philosophers use are designed to probe the language in which our intuitions and beliefs are expressed, and to point out possible confusions, ambiguities, inconsistencies and blurred distinctions – to clarify the concepts we use in formulating statements and arguments, and to examine the justifications we offer for them.

This sounds rather vague and abstract, so let us bring this description of philosophy down to earth, by showing how we can test out the 'moralistic argument' by aiming some philosophical questions at it. If this gives us a clearer picture of what the argument is exactly claiming, how valid it is and what sort of assumptions it rests upon, then philosophy will already have been practically useful in helping us to work out our attitude towards an issue about which teachers cannot avoid holding an opinion.

First, then, what can be said about the claim that standards of behaviour are falling? What sort of a claim is this? It *sounds* like a factual claim – something that we can test *empirically* by going out, collecting data and looking to see if the claim is in fact true. But claiming that standards of behaviour are falling is not like claiming that the temperature, or the birth rate, or inflation is falling. These *are* empirical matters of fact; even if it may be difficult at times for various reasons to ascertain whether a fall is actually occurring, we know *in principle* how to find out and what would make the claim true or false. But what precisely is meant by the claim that standards of behaviour are falling? 'Standards' can mean different things in different contexts: they can, for example, refer either to what is *achieved* or to what is *expected*, so 'standards of behaviour' might indicate either the way in which children are actually behaving, or the way in which adults expect them to behave (Straughan and Wrigley 1980, pp. 12–17). But in either case, what precisely constitutes a 'rise' or a 'fall' in such standards? Is there a universally agreed measure which we can apply to children's behaviour to discover whether its 'standards' are rising or falling?

The difficulty may become more obvious if we take an imaginary example. Suppose that a research project studied a large sample of teenagers in 1978 and a parallel sample in 1988. It observed their behaviour in a variety of contexts, and also set up a battery of tests of the most devious kind (which some psychologists love to use), for example, placing the subjects in situations where they can choose whether or not to cheat, tell the truth, obey instructions, help strangers in apparent distress, and so on. The results of this study, let us imagine, are as follows: the teenagers in 1988, compared with those in 1978, used more bad language, cheated less in examinations, helped fewer old ladies across roads, collected more money for the RSPCA but less for OXFAM, drank more, smoked less, took fewer drugs and were more experienced sexually. Have 'standards of behaviour', then, risen or fallen?

What this example shows is that, when deciding whether

such a rise or fall has occurred, we have first to judge what *counts* as a rise or fall, and not everyone will come to the same conclusion. We can all agree whether the temperature has risen or fallen by observing the thermometer, but mere observation will not settle the question about rising or falling standards of behaviour. This is because we have to make a *moral* judgement in order to give an answer to the latter question, not just attend to the facts of the matter. If, for example, we judge bad language to be a more serious moral issue than cheating, we may decide that standards of teenage behaviour had fallen by 1988; if we judge drug-taking to be morally more reprehensible than ignoring old ladies at kerbsides, then we are likely to conclude that standards had risen. So there can be no simple, empirical method of determining whether standards of behaviour have risen or fallen; it all depends on what one holds to be morally desirable or undesirable, praiseworthy or blame-worthy. Yet the temptation remains to equate morality with *one* specific type of behaviour, and to draw general conclusions about children's moral standards and values by observing the frequency of that behaviour; as was well exemplified in a letter to the *Radio Times*, complaining about an allegedly 'obscene' programme: 'If the BBC want to corrupt the young, they are going the right way about it. Is there no one in the BBC with a sense of moral values? No wonder there are so many children using bad language and having no sense of morals.'

Now this brings us face to face with some of the most fundamental and most difficult questions which philo-sophers try to tackle. What exactly are 'moral values'? How do we make 'moral judgements'? How can we justify calling a particular action right or wrong, good or bad? Are all moral questions a matter of personal opinion, or can we base our moral decisions on more objective grounds? These questions, which the 'moralistic argument' ignores, but which cannot be avoided if we are concerned about 'teaching children to be good', we shall return to in later chapters, but we must at this point briefly note some of the difficulties they create for the 'moralistic argument', which, you will remember, claimed that teachers should take a positive lead in trying to remedy the supposed 'moral vacuum'. This implies that there is an agreed set of answers to all moral questions, and that it is the duty of teachers to ensure that children learn these answers and behave accordingly. Is this an acceptable view?

Clearly, on a number of counts it is not. To begin with, as a matter of sheer fact there *is*, of course, no general agreement on many important moral issues, such as euthanasia, abortion, capital and corporal punishment, civil disobedience, homosexuality, pre-marital sex, and so on. As we have already seen, there seems to be no way of arriving at the 'correct', undisputed answer to a moral question just by looking at the facts of the matter (though this will be examined in much greater detail in Chapter 5).

But even if all or most teachers *were* in agreement over a particular moral issue, would it necessarily follow that their educational duty was to ensure that their pupils acted in accordance with those views? Supposing that a majority of teachers believed that pre-marital sex was wrong, must it be their job as moral educators to teach this belief, and to try to get their pupils to refrain from pre-marital sex? One objection to this sort of approach is that, although it may have various socially desirable effects (in this case, for example, a reduction in teenage abortion and sexually transmitted diseases), its success will depend largely upon pupils conforming and submitting to the consensus view of the teachers, rather than upon them grappling with the moral problem themselves, and gaining a greater understanding of the issues involved.

To put this objection at its simplest, nothing is ever made right by someone *saying* that it is right; moral problems are not solved (morally, at least) by asking someone else what to do, or by merely obeying some authority. Some teachers have difficulty in grasping this point, perhaps because teachers as a group tend to place value upon obedience, compliance and conformity. This is quite understandable, for all teachers need to exercise a considerable degree of social control in doing their job; a teacher's self-confidence and, to some extent, his effectiveness are derived from his belief that the children will do as he tells them, and will conform to the rules of the school. But teaching children to be good is not the same as teaching them to do as they are told; obedience to authority is strictly irrelevant to the business of making moral decisions. Another example should make this clear.

An American psychologist conducted a series of experiments in which members of the public volunteered to take part in what they thought was a study of the effects of punishment upon learning (Milgram 1974). The 'learner', who was in fact an actor, was strapped to a chair and told to learn a list of word pairs. The 'teacher', who was one of the unsuspecting volunteers, was seated in front of what appeared to be an electric shock generator, and was told to administer increasingly severe shocks to the 'learner' each time he gave a wrong answer. The 'learner' in fact received no shocks at all, but pretended to react and protest more and more frenziedly as the level of the shocks apparently increased. If the 'teacher' objected at any point, the person in charge of the experiment would say (in sequence), 'Please continue', or 'The experiment requires that you continue', or 'It is absolutely essential that you continue', or 'You have no other choice, you must go on'. In some of the experiments 65 per cent of the 'teachers' obeyed the experimenter, and went on to inflict what they thought were highly dangerous shocks of 450 volts. It appears, therefore, to be surprisingly and frighteningly easy to induce people to obey an authority, but surely we would not want to say that the 65 per cent of subjects who did as they were told were morally better and more mature than the 35 per cent who refused. Doing something just because you are told to do it, then, has nothing to do with acting morally – a point which will be further amplified in later chapters.

A similar point can be made about the authority of religion, the lack of which, according to the 'moralistic argument', has contributed to the present moral vacuum among youngsters. Rules, commandments and pronouncements which emanate from any religion cannot be morally right just because that religion says so. There is, of course, the further problem that different religions prescribe different rules, drawn from different sacred texts and traditions which purport to reveal the divine will. These often conflict, so how do we decide which particular set of religious prescriptions is morally right? Not by referring back to the religious authority which prescribes it, for that does not solve the difficulty of choosing between *conflicting* religious authorities. We can only test the *moral* worth of religious prescriptions by exercising our own moral judgement upon the issue in question, and making a moral decision about it for ourselves. If we try to short-cut the problem by saying 'It must be right because the Bible says so' (or the Koran, or the Pope, or the Chief Rabbi, or the local witch-doctor, or the guru, or any other religious authority), we are again equating the making of a moral decision with doing as we are told.

So it must be mistaken to assume that the so-called 'moral vacuum' can be filled simply by schools placing more emphasis upon religion in order to provide children with authoritative answers about how they ought to behave. That sort of approach might or might not change children's behaviour in various ways, but the result could not be called *moral* behaviour if the children were merely conforming to the 'right answers' laid down by an (in this case religious) authority. Much more, however, needs to be said about the precise characteristics of moral behaviour and moral reasoning, and this will form a major part of the following chapters.

To conclude this introductory chapter, let us now turn our attention to another very hazy aspect of the 'moralistic argument'. If teachers are expected to take more of a 'moral lead' in schools, what exactly will this amount to, in terms of actual teaching activities and methods? The 'moralistic argument' seems to assume that all problems will disappear as soon as teachers become sufficiently concerned about 'falling standards of behaviour'. But even if teachers do consider it part of their job to teach children to be good, there then arise not only questions about *what* to teach, as we have already seen, but also questions about *how* to teach it, whatever it is.

What sort of teaching is the teacher here being expected to do? Is he being asked to teach children *that certain things are true* (as the geography teacher might teach that Rome is the capital of Italy)? Or to teach children *how to do certain things* (as the mathematics teacher might teach a class how to solve quadratic equations)? Or to teach children *to do certain things* (as the science teacher might teach pupils to be careful when handling dangerous chemicals)? The answer will depend upon what the appropriate subject matter of 'moral education' is considered to be, and we have already seen how the complexities of that question were ignored in the 'moralistic argument'. In fact, a case can probably be made for the inclusion of all three types of teaching, as will be shown in Chapter 6, which suggests that there may well be no simple, unitary method of 'teaching children to be good'.

Moreover, by failing to recognize the different forms of teaching which may be involved in moral education, the 'moralistic argument' blurs another distinction, which results in the teacher's difficulties being further under-estimated. Teaching children *to do* X is directly related to the particular behaviour (X) which results; for example, I can claim that I have successfully taught a child to tell the truth at all times, only if the child, as a result of my teaching, *does* in fact tell the truth at all times. But teaching *that* . . . and teaching *how* . . . are not so directly tied to the child's behaviour in this way (Scheffler 1960, ch. V) If I successfully teach a child *that* it is wrong to steal, he will have learned *that* it is wrong to steal, but that is no guarantee that he *will not* steal on some future occasion. Similarly, if I teach a child *how* to handle fireworks safely, he will have learned *how* to handle fireworks safely, but again there is no guarantee that he *will* handle his fireworks safely on Bonfire Night. Not all forms of teaching and learning, then, necessarily lead to the required pattern of behaviour, for the propositions and skills that are taught and learned (in the 'that' and 'how' forms) may for various reasons not always be put into practice by the learner. So, by equating moral education with teaching children *to* behave in certain ways, and by ignoring the other less direct forms of teaching which may nevertheless also be important, the 'moralistic argument' makes the teacher's job sound far more simple and more assured of success than it really is.

This notion of teaching children to behave in specified

ways, and the certainty of outcome which it suggests, create yet more problems for the 'moralistic argument' on closer inspection. There are numerous ways of ensuring that people behave in a required manner, but the more certain and predictable the behaviour becomes, the less appropriate does it seem to talk of 'teaching'. Conditioning techniques, for example, can be used with both animals and human beings to produce specific forms of behaviour in response to specific stimuli. But can this sort of method, where the outcome is certain and where the learner is left no freedom of choice or decision, properly be called 'teaching'? Furthermore, if the result is inevitable, can we even say that the person is *acting*, rather than being caused to behave in a particular way? These questions will be followed up in greater detail in Chapter 3, but the point must be made here that 'teaching' surely suggests, among other things, an attempt to achieve learning by offering to pupils good reasons for believing certain things and for acting in certain ways (Scheffler 1960, ch. III). But one cannot *compel* anyone to accept such reasons as the basis for his beliefs and behaviour; and even if the reasons are accepted as good ones by the learner, it does not necessarily follow that he will choose to *act* upon those reasons. There can, then, be no direct or certain method of 'teaching children to be good', for no teacher can guarantee to make a child accept and act upon reasons, in the way that one can guarantee to make a person sneeze by giving him too much snuff, or a sheepdog sit by giving the appropriate command.

We have seen, then, that the 'moralistic argument', which 'sounded right' in many respects, soon begins to show signs of inadequacy and even incoherence when it is subjected to some critical probing. This probing, however, has so far been superficial and unsystematic, although a number of key issues have already emerged which no teacher can afford to ignore. Is it in fact part of the duty of all teachers to 'teach children to be good'? Is such teaching feasible and desirable? What can be said about the precise aims of this enterprise? What should form its subject matter? What methods can and should be used?

One way of starting to tackle these complex questions is to

look at how current educational theory and practice are facing up to them, and at what is actually going on in schools within this area. Such an approach is unlikely to provide us with all the answers, and may even raise more problems than it solves, but it will at least set our investigation within a practical and topical context and so keep us in firm contact with educational reality.

2: What Are the Main Approaches to Moral Education?

Education has always been thought to contain an essential 'moral' component. It is a straightforward, though laborious, task to list the pronouncements of great thinkers on the subject, ranging from Plato nearly 2,500 years ago in Athens, to the anonymous authors of recent D.E.S. and H.M.I. reports, but a detailed historical survey is not the concern of this book.

Recent approaches and developments within the area of moral education, however, do serve to illustrate the complexity of the problems raised in Chapter 1, as a recent American writer has observed:

> The American educator has always been a moral educator. Whether from the austere Puritan or the indulgent romantic, children have traditionally received moral training. What is new about current perspectives on moral education is not their explicit concern for morality but their awareness of moral complexity.
> (Hersh, Miller and Fielding 1980, p. 25)

The best way of examining this complexity, then, is probably to review briefly what approaches to moral education have been most influential in recent years and what objections have been raised against them. This should provide us with a variety of viewpoints on what might be meant by teaching children to be good.

2.1 Value transmission

This label is intended to cover the many everyday procedures which teachers adopt, often perhaps without a great deal of reflection, in order to influence children's beliefs and behaviour, and which underlie the frequently voiced claim that 'all teachers are really teachers of moral education'. It is certainly true that all teachers in their interactions with individuals, groups and classes are inevitably seen to support certain values by their encouragement or discouragement of certain forms of behaviour. Thus, one teacher may, by what he says and does, what he rewards and punishes, what he smiles and frowns at, indicate the importance he places upon the values of, say, truthfulness, perseverance and keeping a stiff upper lip, while another may similarly emphasize the virtues of considerateness, tolerance and patience. More formally, the school as an institution will, again inevitably, underline certain values rather than others as a result of the particular style of discipline it maintains and the rules which it enforces.

There is, needless to say, nothing particularly new about this form of 'moral education'. It is, for example, a characteristic deeply embedded in the tradition of the English public school, described in a recent sociological analysis as follows:

> It was their moral, rather than their academic curriculum for which these schools became famous. The desired qualities were consciously taught mainly outside formal lessons. In school chapel they were joined to the power of an old and powerful religious tradition; more particularly, the pupils' future role as leaders at home and in the Empire was set in the spirit of Christian sacrifice. On the games field, the vocabulary of motives, hinted at in Newbolt's poem, was learnt. This was concerned, for example, with playing the game, obeying the rules, and taking punishment like a man...
>
> (Musgrave 1978, p. 64)

Grammar and elementary schools in the first half of this

century were also strongly influenced by this conception of 'moral education'. Musgrave, for example, also refers to Morant's *Handbook of Suggestions for the Consideration of Teachers and others concerned in the Work of the Public Elementary Schools* (1905), which declared:

> The everyday incidents of school life will enable the teachers to impress upon the scholars the importance of punctuality, of good manners and language, of cleanliness and neatness, of cheerful obedience to duty, of consideration and respect for others, and of honour and truthfulness in word and act.
>
> (Musgrave 1978, pp. 67–8)

This is certainly not a novel approach to moral education, therefore, as teachers have always attempted to transmit values to their pupils. What must be considered as a significant recent development, however, has been the growing recognition that teachers and schools may be to a greater or lesser extent self-consciously *aware* of their inevitable role as value-transmitters. Some teachers may, perhaps in accordance with the explicit aims of the school, deliberately and consistently attempt to transmit values A, B, C, while others may in fact be transmitting those values much more effectively but without being aware of it, possibly imagining that they are really transmitting values X, Y, Z. Obviously the ways in which teachers behave towards each other and towards pupils can have a powerful influence upon those pupils' own moral attitudes, as can such factors as school organization, its rituals and traditions. Recent theorists have tried to make this rather common-sensical point far more mysterious and sinister than it really is by introducing the notion of the 'hidden curriculum', which is both confused and confusing; a curriculum refers, by definition, to an *intentional* programme of educational activities, whereas if the 'hidden curriculum' is really as hidden as some writers imply, no one could ever be aware of it at all or do anything to modify it. Nevertheless, this realization that teachers and schools can exert a powerful, unintended influence upon pupils' beliefs, attitudes and behaviour, has caused many teachers to reflect upon their role as value-transmitters and also has led, by way of reaction, to a very different and more distinctive approach to moral education.

2.2 Value neutrality

This approach was pioneered by the Schools Council Nuffield Humanities Project, which was initiated in 1967 under the directorship of Lawrence Stenhouse, its aim being to 'develop an understanding of social situations and human acts and of the controversial value issues they raise'. Controversial issues were to be handled in the classroom with adolescents, but the teacher's role was not to provide authoritative 'answers'. Instead, he was to act as a neutral chairman, feeding in as evidence various kinds of written and pictorial material to discussions on such topics as war, education, poverty, law and order, and relations between the sexes. The rationale of the Project and its concern to avoid teachers acting as moral authorities are well summed up in its major premises:

1 that controversial issues should be handled in the classroom with adolescents;
2 that the teacher accepts the need to submit his teaching in controversial areas to the criterion of neutrality at this stage of education, i.e. that he regards it as part of his responsibility not to promote his own view;
3 that the mode of enquiry in controversial areas should have discussion, rather than instruction, as its core;
4 that the discussion should protect divergence of view among participants, rather than attempt to achieve consensus;
5 that the teacher as chairman of the discussion should have responsibility for quality and standards in learning.

(Schools Council 1970, p. 1)

This approach, however, interest in which persisted

throughout the 1970s and has recently revived again in the mid-1980s, has proved to be as controversial as the issues it suggests for debate. There has been much disagreement over whether such neutrality is possible in the classroom, and if so whether it is morally and educationally desirable (e.g. Taylor 1975, Section 2). Perhaps the strongest objection from the viewpoint of moral education is that voiced by Mary Warnock. 'The teacher must be a *leader* in argument if he is to teach argument,' she maintains (1975, p. 165). It follows, then, that he must demonstrate to pupils how moral arguments are conducted and moral conclusions drawn, for it is educationally important that children 'must not be deprived of the spectacle of a teacher who holds, and clearly expresses, moral views' (p. 170).

2.3 Values clarification

This approach, which has made considerable impact in America and Canada in recent years, bears some resemblance to the previous one, for the teacher is again called upon to avoid 'moralising, criticising, giving values or evaluating' (Raths, Harmin and Simon 1966, p. 53). The aim is for the individual pupil to 'get in touch with his own values, to bring them to the surface, and to reflect upon them' (Purpel and Ryan 1976, p. 73). By focusing on the process of valuing, it is claimed, confusion about values will be reduced and a clearer direction given to life. This process of valuing involves the following stages:

Choosing (1) freely
                (2) from alternatives
                (3) after thoughtful consideration of the consequences of each alternative.
Prizing (4) cherishing, being happy with the choice
                (5) enough to be willing to affirm the choice to others.
Acting (6) or doing something with the choice
                (7) repeatedly in some pattern of life
(Raths *et al.* 1966, p. 28)

To aid this valuing process a wide variety of teaching

materials has been devised, some of which have found their way into British classrooms. Much use is made of games, simulation exercises and discussion. A typical example of a values-clarification activity would be for the teacher to say:

> Take out three things from your wallet (or purse) that show three different things you value. These three items can be anything at all; the mere fact that you carry them in your wallet says something. Place the three items on your desk and begin thinking about what you will tell us about what any or all of them mean to you and your value system.
>
> (Simon, Howe and Kirschenbaum 1972, p. 329)

But is it enough, morally or educationally, just to *clarify* what one values? A variety of objections has been levelled against this approach, most of them attacking the relativistic view of morality which it implies. If one focuses exclusively on the *process* of valuing, then 'if one uses the process, whatever values one arrives at are all right' (Shaver and Strong 1982, p. 143). Or, as Fraenkel puts it, to teach that 'self-awareness is an end in itself' is to teach that 'all values are the same, that no value is better than any other – only "different"' (1977, p. 45). Values clarification, then, raises some fundamental questions about the nature of moral values, to which we shall have to return a little later.

2.4 The development of consideration

No attempt at 'neutrality' or mere 'clarification' is made by the next approach, which declares its aim to be to encourage boys and girls to 'live well' and to adopt a 'considerate style of life'. This was the approach developed by the Schools Council Moral Education Project under the leadership of Peter McPhail (McPhail, Ungoed-Thomas and Chapman 1972) which produced a variety of teaching materials under the title of 'Lifeline'. These materials present situations of varying degrees of complexity, ranging from problems of interpersonal relationships at home, school or in the local neighbourhood ('In Other People's Shoes'), to more complex issues of group interests and authority ('Proving the Rule'), and finally to broader social dilemmas involving such matters as pacifism, racial discrimination and drug addiction ('What Would You have Done?'). By using and discussing these graded materials in various ways (e.g. in role play, socio-drama, play-writing and painting), it is claimed that adolescents will learn to become more sensitive to other people's needs and interests, to predict the consequences of actions and to develop greater overall social awareness.

After ten years' use in secondary schools the materials were updated. There also appeared in 1978 an additional set of materials entitled 'Startline', devised for children of 8–13 years, which placed a similar emphasis upon the development of interpersonal understanding and empathy.

Despite its interesting materials the Project's underlying theoretical basis has been criticized on a number of grounds. Can considerateness, for example, be set up as the sole aim of moral education, or as the sole principle of morality? Furthermore, the Project claims to have discovered this principle from a pilot study which questioned a sample of teenagers about what they considered to be examples of 'good' and 'bad' behaviour; but the opinions of a few hundred schoolchildren can hardly be used to erect a whole theory of morality and moral education upon, for an opinion poll can only demonstrate what people think, not what is morally desirable or praiseworthy. These points will be elaborated further in Chapter 5.

2.5 The development of moral reasoning

The most detailed and influential work on moral development in recent years has undoubtedly been that of the American psychologist, Lawrence Kohlberg, and his associates. This work and its implications for moral education will again be referred to later in this book, but what is needed at this point is a brief indication of Kohlberg's contribution as an alternative approach to the practice of moral education.

Kohlberg claims that in any culture individuals progress through a set pattern of stages in their moral development.

Our reasoning about moral situations gradually becomes more complex and sophisticated, as we move from the Preconventional level (where one might judge the rightness or wrongness of an action in terms of the reward or punishment it attracts) to the Conventional level (where the demands of rules and authority become the overriding moral criterion), and finally (though not for everybody) to the Postconventional or Principled level (where more general ethical principles concerning justice and individual rights come into play). So what determines the level of moral development a person is at is not the particular *action* he judges to be right or wrong, but his *reasons* for so judging (Kohlberg 1984, Part One).

Kohlberg has elucidated these different stages of reasoning by analysing people's responses to a variety of hypothetical moral dilemmas, the best known of which is the 'Heinz dilemma' which poses the question of whether it could ever be morally right to steal a drug in order to save a life. These dilemmas can also be used as materials for moral education in schools as well as for psychological research and testing, for one of Kohlberg's most interesting claims is that it is possible to 'accelerate' people's moral development by engaging them in discussion of such dilemmas in which they encounter reasoning of a higher level than their own. Another context in which Kohlberg believes that 'acceleration' can take place is that of the 'just community' or the 'school within a school', where the educational institution itself is modified in order to involve pupils directly in democratic, decision-making procedures (1984, pp. 263–70).

Objections to the Kohlbergian approach are many and varied (see e.g. Modgil and Modgil 1986), but at this point we need only note that this approach to moral education places great emphasis upon the development and acceleration of moral *reasoning*. This presupposes:

(a) that the stage-theory is correct,
and
(b) that the sort of reasoning which distinguishes the stages is the *central* feature of morality and moral education.

Needless to say, both of these presuppositions can be challenged.

It should be noted that in his later work Kohlberg seems radically to change his mind about the implications of his theory for moral education, conceding that the moral educator 'deals with concrete morality in a school world in which value content as well as structure, behaviour as well as reasoning, must be dealt with ... The educator must be a socializer, teaching value content and behaviour, not merely a Socratic facilitator of development' (1978, p. 84). This apparent recantation would not be accepted by all of Kohlberg's followers, but it must cast further doubts upon the 'development of moral reasoning' approach to moral education (see Locke 1987).

2.6 *Values across the curriculum*

This approach to moral education is probably the one which most teachers would be most ready to accept and support. The previous five approaches (with the possible exception of the first) all imply that moral education can be seen in some respects as a distinct, educational enterprise which teachers, perhaps with some specific expertise, are to undertake *in addition to* their other curricular concerns. But just as it can be argued that 'language' permeates the teaching of all subject areas, and hence should be taught 'across the curriculum', so can a similar policy be advocated for 'morals'. The rationale for this approach rests upon the claim that all (or most) school subjects already possess a 'moral dimension' of some kind and that thorough subject-teaching will accordingly offer a more natural and appropriate medium for moral education than a separate, timetabled course on the subject (if indeed such a subject can be distinguished and taught). The main objections to this approach, however, are that:

(i)   there is no guarantee that all teachers will pay sufficient attention to the 'moral dimension' of the subject they are teaching, and

(ii) it is arguable that moral education requires as much

specialist knowledge and methodological expertise as any other subject, and that it is consequently unrealistic to expect all teachers to be automatically competent at handling moral issues in the classroom.

This alleged 'moral dimension' enters into different subjects in different ways, and some curriculum areas are more obvious candidates for this kind of treatment than others. Let us consider a brief selection.

Religious Education is seen by many teachers, parents and politicians as having an essentially moral function. Indeed, historically instruction in religion was usually thought to provide a *sufficient* basis for children's moral upbringing, and even the Plowden Report on Primary Education in 1967 (normally considered a landmark of progressive educational thinking) recommended that 'children should be brought up to know and love God and to practise in the school community the virtues appropriate to their age and environment' (para. 572). More recently, developments in religious education have led to a diminishing emphasis upon biblical study and a corresponding increase of activity on two fronts, both exhibiting a clear 'moral dimension':

1 a study of other world religions in addition to Christianity, often with the aim of developing a more informed and sympathetic understanding of our own modern multicultural society.
2 an examination of current moral and social issues (e.g. war, racism, labour relations, euthanasia, animal rights, etc.) from a variety of religious perspectives.

History, Geography and Social Studies can be given a similar kind of 'moral dimension' in the area of interpersonal understanding. History offers opportunities to examine human motives and intentions, while geography and social studies can illustrate differences of culture and lifestyle. The moral objective here would be to enlarge and refine children's concept of a 'person', and perhaps to improve their ability to put themselves into other persons' shoes.

English, in particular literature and drama, is likewise often claimed to have an important function in the development of empathy and moral sensitivity. The Bullock Report, *A Language for Life* (1975) summed up these claims as follows:

> In Britain the tradition of literature teaching is one which aims at personal and moral growth, and in the last two decades this emphasis has grown. It is a soundly based tradition, and properly interpreted is a powerful force in English teaching. Literature brings the child into an encounter with language in its most complex and varied forms. Through these complexities are presented the thoughts, experiences, and feelings of people who exist outside and beyond the reader's daily awareness. This process of bringing them within that circle of consciousness is where the greatest value of literature lies. It provides imaginative insight into what another person is feeling; it allows the contemplation of possible human experiences which the reader himself has not met. It has the capacity to develop that empathy of which Shelley was speaking when he said: 'man to be greatly good, must imagine intensively and comprehensively; he must put himself in the place of another and many others; the pains and pleasures of his species must become his own. (p. 125)

Yet the Report also sounded a sceptical note as to 'whether literature does in fact make the reader a better and more sensitive human being' (p. 124), for as Sampson observed over fifty years ago, 'Reading Blake to a class is not going to turn boys into saints' (1921).

Science is another curriculum area which can readily be given a 'moral dimension', for it is undeniable that scientific discoveries and technological developments can and do raise serious moral problems. Can atomic physics, therefore, be taught without due attention being paid to the moral issues concerning the use of nuclear power? Can biology teachers avoid discussion of the morality of genetic engineering? The answer in both cases is, of course, 'Yes', for many science teachers would argue that science is strictly 'value-free', and that it is the *use* to which scientific knowledge is put which creates the moral issues, not the activity of science itself. Yet it is probably true that an increasing number of science teachers would reject this sharp distinction, feeling under some educational obligation to deal with the moral implications of the subject they are teaching.

2.7 Personal and social education

This currently fashionable addition to the curriculum of many schools is probably best viewed not so much as a possible *approach* to moral education but as a synonym (or even euphemism) for it. In practice it can include any or all of the six approaches already described above. 'Personal' and 'social' seem to be more acceptable adjectives than 'moral' at present, though it is the contention of this book that 'moral' is a term which leads to less educational confusion. Part of the stimulus for this linguistic shift came from such educational reports as the *Secondary Survey* (1979) which stated, 'It has become the practice that schools should design courses which contribute to personal and social development', devoting a whole chapter to the area, while 'A View of the Curriculum' (1980) spoke of 'personal and social development in the broad sense' as being 'a major change on the curriculum'. In addition, the Assessment of Performance Unit set up an exploratory group in 1976 to investigate the desirability and feasibility of monitoring children's personal and social development. The group started from 'the generally agreed viewpoint that pupils' personal and social development is given the highest priority by teachers, both in school organisation and in curriculum design', though the assessment proposals were abandoned in 1980.

So vague and all-embracing a label as 'personal and social education', however, inevitably creates problems, which have been neatly pinpointed by Pring as follows:

Presumably the English teacher introducing *Middle-march*, the history teacher dealing with the social consequences of the Civil War, the R.E. teacher explaining various religious ideals, the house tutor helping a pupil through some emotional difficulty, the P.E. teacher persuading the rugger team to grit their teeth in the face of fierce opposition – all would claim with justification to be contributing to the personal and social development of the pupils. How can one make coherent curriculum sense out of such a wide range of classroom activities, teaching objectives, sought-for skills, attitudes, habits, values?

(1982, p. 136)

The main problem in fact with 'personal and social education' is that it is at once too broad and too narrow a notion to do the job for which it is intended. It is too broad in that *all* education, if it is really to qualify for that title, must be both 'personal' and 'social': it is personal in the sense that education must *change* persons – in particular, their personal attitudes, beliefs and perspectives – and social in the sense that it takes place within a social context and is designed to fulfil various social purposes. However, the label is also too narrow in that it fails to make specific reference to the *moral* element which must be central to it. A few examples will illustrate this latter point, which is of extreme importance.

Programmes of personal and social education tend to lay great emphasis upon the development of 'personal and social skills', 'self-knowledge', 'social awareness', 'life skills' and similar impressive-sounding objectives, without appearing to realize that these all need an explicit *moral* foundation if they are to function as acceptable and justifiable educational aims. Ruthless dictators, manipulative politicians and cunning confidence-tricksters will score very highly on these counts; it is such people's personal and social skills, knowledge and awareness which further their successful careers. These are not of course the sort of people which personal and social education is hoping to produce, but there is nothing to rule them out as exemplars of such education unless we become less coy about using the word 'moral' and admit that personal and social education is really aimed at *particular* personal and social goals which are deemed to be desirable – *morally* desirable. These goals will inevitably express a set of moral values and underline certain moral priorities rather than others; and as will be shown in later chapters, any such values and priorities are always open to challenge and debate and can never be laid down as unquestionably 'true' or 'right'.

Let us take just one recent example from the fast-growing literature on personal and social education to show the sort of confusion that can be generated by this terminology. *Developing Social Awareness in Young Children* (Goodall *et al.* 1983, Exeter Workbooks in Education, No. 4) is a workbook which is described as 'arising out of the experiences of a group of teachers' and is the kind of material which is commonly used on in-service courses in this area. It begins by asking 'What is social awareness?' and answers this key question by suggesting:

> A socially aware child is one who is co-operative, is able to share, shows self-control, has a good self-concept, cares for property and natural surroundings, shows empathy, knows that her/his behaviour affects others, takes the intentions of others into account . . . (p. 9)

But this is not, of course, what 'social awareness' *means*. A socially aware child is one who, if we are to respect normal language usage, is aware of and has some understanding of social forces, factors and conditions; he realizes that human beings interact in various interesting ways and do not operate simply as isolated individuals. Such awareness, however, does not necessarily mean that that child is co-operative, able to share, self-controlled, and the rest; he might be selfish, intolerant, acquisitive and unsympathetic.

The suggested definition in the workbook, then, is not *describing* what a 'socially aware' child is; it is *prescribing* what those offering the definition think that a 'socially aware' child *ought* to be. A particular set of moral values and priorities is being smuggled in with no open acknowledgement that they are indeed *moral*. And however much most of us might approve of those values and priorities they remain open to challenge and debate – a thorough-going Marxist, for example, might not be too keen on 'care for property'.

Personal and social education, therefore, does not avoid any of the many problems raised by moral education simply by avoiding mention of the word 'moral'. Recent interest in personal and social education has at least had the effect of concentrating attention upon curricular questions of method and content in this area, but by using this terminology teachers and educationists may be deluded into thinking that they no longer have to face the task of teaching children to be good.

Pring's question about how to make 'coherent curriculum sense' of personal and social education can also be asked more generally of the whole range of approaches which have been outlined in this chapter. What 'coherence', if any, can be detected between these approaches? Do they share any underlying rationale and any common aims and objectives, or do they represent a set of unrelated and perhaps incompatible conceptions of morality and assumptions about children's moral development? Are all of these approaches really concerned with something that can properly be called 'moral education'? On the face of it, at least, the various educational recommendations, developments and practices which we have noted in this section seem to make up a fairly motley assortment, so confirming the view of one well-known writer on the subject that 'moral education is the name for nothing clear' (Wilson 1967, p. 11). What does emerge clearly from this section, however, is that the traditional emphasis upon the moral element of education is still evident in many aspects of current educational theory and practice. The present picture is nevertheless an undeniably confused one, and we must try in the next chapter to dispel some of this confusion by looking more closely at 'morality' and 'goodness', following Plato's strategy of making 'a determined attack on virtue itself and its essential nature' before returning to the question of whether or not it can be taught.

3: What Does It Mean To Be Good?

Already we have seen that the question whether or not we can teach children to be good is far more complex than it at first appears. Part of this complexity stems from the fact that the question is really a double-barrelled one, each element needing separate consideration before any answer can be attempted. On the one hand, there is the problem of what exactly is meant by 'being good', and what exactly 'goodness' of this kind consists of; and on the other hand, there is the problem of how, if at all, this 'goodness' can be taught to children. Both of these problems have been illustrated in Chapters 1 and 2, but we must now begin to examine them in much greater depth, concentrating upon the various issues which they raise, and the wide diversity of views which philosophers and educationalists have held about them. Only after clearing the ground in this way shall we be able to stand back and offer a reasonably informed and comprehensive response to our original question. Let us make a start, then, by considering what might be meant when we speak of children 'being good'.

3.1 Goodness and morality

The meaning of 'good' and 'goodness' can hardly be properly established in a few introductory paragraphs, for philosophers and others have been filling libraries with their deliberations on this subject for centuries. We shall, therefore, have to be selective here in focusing upon those philosophical questions about 'goodness' which are of the most direct relevance to teachers concerned with the behaviour of children and with the possibility of 'moral education'.

The first and most obvious point to make is that 'goodness' is a very general term, and that it is one particular type of 'goodness' only to which we need pay attention. People in general and children in particular may be called 'good' on many different counts and in many different contexts: they may be designated good losers, or good eaters, or good mixers, or good students, for example, implying that they have reached some desired standard of achievement or proficiency in those activities, and are thereby judged to be good *at* them. But the type of goodness that we are trying to pin down is best described as *moral* goodness, and although this must also involve coming up to some kind of standard, we do not usually think of a person who is called morally good as being good *at* something, in quite the way that we think a good tennis-player or car-mechanic is. Much more will need to be said about this later for, as we shall seen, some philosophers and educationalists have in fact tried to analyse moral goodness in terms of distinct moral *skills* and *abilities* (which one *can* be relatively good or bad at). However, in ordinary language it is fair to say that calling a person morally good carries with it different implications from those conveyed in calling him good *at* some activity, as the ascription of moral goodness does not need or invite any further elaboration in the way that ascriptions of other kinds of goodness do. If you were to tell me that Mary is a good girl, or that she is being very good today, you would be surprised if I were to reply; 'Oh yes, and what is she being good at?' And the reason for your surprise would be that you were obviously referring to *moral* goodness, which seemed to make my question odd and inappropriate; the moral goodness of Mary is in a sense self-contained and an end in itself, not needing to be spelt out in terms of something *else* that Mary is good *at*.

This does not mean, of course, that we cannot explain and expand upon why we believe someone to be morally good by pointing to reasons which we think justify our belief. But these reasons may be of widely varying kinds, and the question then arises as to which reasons can and which cannot be accepted as an indisputable indication of moral goodness. Let us look at some examples of claims that might be made by proud parents or teachers about their children's 'goodness'.

(a) Jane is a good girl. She always does as she's told.

(b) John is a good boy. He never argues or answers back.

(c) Jill is a good girl. She's always ready to help anyone in trouble.

(d) Jonathan is a good boy. He's always so worried if he feels he's done anything wrong.

(e) Jean is a good girl. She never misses a Sunday school class.

(f) Jason is a good boy. He's never been in trouble with the police.

(g) Joan is a good girl. She never skips her homework.

(h) Jim is a good boy. He's always so upset if anyone else is unhappy.

(i) June is a good girl. She always does what's right without having to think about it.

(j) James is a good boy. He means well – though he often gets led astray.

(k) Janine is a good girl. If she believes something ought to be done, she'll not rest until she's done it.

What do these accounts of children's moral goodness have in common? Not much, as far as the detailed justifications are concerned, but at a more general level they are all telling us some facts about the child in question, attributing (implicitly) moral value or virtue to those facts, and drawing the conclusion that the child is, therefore, 'good'. They are all describing a certain state of affairs, and at the same time expressing approval of it, which is partly at least how we make moral evaluations in our everyday lives.

But can all of the above examples in fact qualify as possible instances of moral goodness? Surely not *any* behaviour which we happen to approve of and praise can properly count as 'moral' behaviour. I may approve of and praise Botham's powerful stroke-play, or Bonnington's mountaineering technique, or Bergman's camera work, without any *moral* evaluations entering in. We have first to decide whether the behaviour is of any moral significance, and whether it involves any moral considerations of moral issues, before we can bestow the accolade of moral *goodness* upon it. To take a couple of parallel instances, we cannot praise a person for his scientific brilliance unless we are first sure that he is engaged in scientific work, nor can we commend a person's historical acumen unless we are first sure that he is working on historical questions. The area of a person's activities and concerns has to be demarcated before we can apply the appropriate standards to them and make the appropriate evaluations. So, in order to be able to exhibit moral goodness, one must first be operating as a moral agent within the moral area, and as we shall see shortly, it is by no means clear which of the children in the examples *(a) - (k)* are doing this.

Obviously, then, we need to sort out what might be meant by 'operating as a moral agent within the moral area' before we can make any assessment of a child's moral goodness. It is important here to grasp a crucial distinction which has already been implied in the foregoing remarks, and which can lead to all kinds of confusion if ignored.

The word 'moral' is used in two different ways. Firstly, it is used virtually as the equivalent of 'morally good': that is, to assign a particular sort of value and standard to persons, actions, intentions, policies and decisions, and to express a particular sort of approval of these. By using 'moral' in this sense, which can be called the *evaluative* sense, one necessarily reveals some of one's *own* values and priorities, as the speakers in examples *(a) - (k)* were doing. In fact, in each of those examples the word 'moral' (used evaluatively) could be substituted for the word 'good', for all the speakers are making judgements of value, and in so doing are telling us something about themselves as well as about the children – that they approve of obedience, or keeping out of trouble, or helping other people, or whatever.

Secondly, however, 'moral' can be used in a *descriptive* sense, when its function is simply to describe what we referred to above as 'the moral area' – that is, a particular category of issues, concerns and activities distinguishable from other categories which serve to pick out, say, the scientific, or the artistic, or the political, or the religious area. What exactly the distinguishing characteristics of the moral area are is a difficult question, which will be investigated at some length in this and the following chapters, but we do in practice accept that such an area exists and can be contrasted with the non-moral area. In the field of sex education, for instance, we have to distinguish between moral questions about how sexual relationships are to be conducted and non-moral questions about how conception occurs. 'Moral' in its descriptive sense, then, merely defines the limits within which 'operations in the moral area' can take place.

To illustrate further how these two senses of 'moral' function and are at times confused, let us return to example *(a):* 'Jane is a good girl. She always does as she's told.' The speaker here, if questioned further, would no doubt agree that it is Jane's *moral* goodness that is being referred to, so Jane is in effect being praised for being 'moral' in the evaluative sense, because she always does as she is told. But someone might object to this (particularly if he had just read in Chapter 1 of this book that mere obedience has nothing to do with morality) by asking: 'What's moral about doing as you're told?' This would not imply that he was morally *disapproving* of doing as you are told; his point would be not that obedience as such is *immoral* (evaluatively), but that it is *non-moral* (descriptively) – just as an ability to wiggle one's ears or recite the alphabet backwards is a *non-moral* matter.

Confusion between the two senses of 'moral' is particularly evident in debates and disputes about 'moral education'. Those who support some form of the 'moralistic argument', for instance, will tend to use 'moral' only in its evaluative sense, and to assume that moral education must, by definition, aim at producing behaviour in children which they, as adults, value as being morally good; so on this evaluative interpretation, if I believe it to be morally good to obey adults' instructions unquestioningly at all times, I

shall consider the achievement of this behaviour necessarily
to be one of the goals of moral education, and one of the
indications of its effectiveness. But if 'moral' is taken in its
descriptive sense, 'moral education' becomes a different
activity with different objectives, for it will now be
concerned with introducing children to the moral field of
operations; so, on the descriptive interpretation, 'moral
education' will be judged to have succeeded (in part at least)
if children are made more aware of the existence of the moral
area – if their understanding of moral issues and problems is
increased, and their grasp of moral arguments and moral
language is improved. 'Moral education', then, can be seen
either as (evaluatively) prescribing a certain version and
pattern of moral goodness for children to adopt, or as
(descriptively) introducing children to the complexities of a
new and distinctive area of experience; so it is easy to
imagine how a discussion of the aims and methods of moral
education in which the participants rely upon different
senses of 'moral' to argue their point (probably without
realizing that there *are* these different senses) can get nowhere
very quickly indeed. Most of the approaches described
in Chapter 2 fall into one or other of these categories of
'moral education' – value transmission and the development
of consideration, for example, would be largely evaluative,
while value neutrality and the development of moral
reasoning would be largely descriptive.

Whether either or both of these forms of moral education
should actually be attempted must be left as an open
question at this stage. However, *if* either or both forms are
attempted, it follows that the descriptive version must have
some sort of priority, because the evaluative version is largely
dependent upon it. As has already been noted, we must first
know roughly what can count (descriptively) as a moral
matter before we can make coherent judgements (evaluatively) about what is morally good or bad. So children must
similarly have some idea of the features and range of moral
operations before we can recommend to them a particular
pattern of moral goodness which they will recognize *as* an
example of moral goodness. There is little point in
preaching the virtue of keeping one's promises to a young

child who does not understand the convention of promise-making and the moral implications which surround it.

If we are, then, to probe further into the notions of 'moral goodness' and 'moral education', we must start by considering the descriptive sense of 'moral', for we need to be clearer about the nature of morality before we can turn to the problem of whether we should teach children that X is morally better or worse than Y. In practice, we shall probably find that there are often close connections between the two uses of 'moral', for there is much disagreement over what constitutes, descriptively, the nature of morality, and these different views can often lead to different judgements about what is morally good and bad.

Investigating the nature of morality is very much the business of moral philosophy or ethics. One of the main functions of philosophy in general is to stand back from some area of activity or study (such as morality, or politics, or education, or science, or religion, or history, or psychology, or art), and ask questions about its features and characteristics. What are the area's boundaries? (When does a religious question begin to raise moral issues?) What distinguishes one area from another? (How is a scientific judgement different from an artistic one?) How is argument and reasoning conducted within an area? (How does one set about establishing and testing an educational, or political, or historical theory?) What kind of language and concepts are distinctive of an area, and how are they used? (What is meant by 'duty', 'rights' and 'obligations' in morality, or 'drive', 'stage' and 'ego' in psychology?)

Because philosophy stands back and analyses in this way, it has sometimes been called a 'second-order activity', meaning that it operates upon an already established subject or activity in an almost parasitic kind of way: without the existence of science, scientists, scientific knowledge, scientific theories and scientific procedures, for example, there could be no philosophy of science, asking 'second-order' questions about the nature of science, because there would be no 'first-order' scientific goings-on to ask questions about. Another helpful description of philosophy, which makes a similar point, is that it is concerned with 'logical geography': that is, it surveys an area, such as one of those mentioned in the previous paragraph, and tries to map it out in a special way, by drawing in its logical features. These are those fundamental characteristics which make the area what it is, and without which it could not exist in the same form (for example, part of what is *meant* by a 'scientific' approach is that it is an attempt to solve problems by testing hypotheses through controlled experiments, rather than by consulting an astrologer or an oracle).

Philosophers, then, should have something useful to say about the descriptive sense of 'moral' and of 'moral education', which we need to clarify before we can reach any conclusions about teaching children to be morally good. Moral philosophy (a term which itself exemplifies the descriptive use of 'moral') performs the 'second-order' function of standing back and studying the characteristic features of moral judgements and behaviour, moral reasoning and argument, moral principles and concepts; in this way, it tries among other things to work out the 'logical geography' of morality. Or, to use another analogy, we might think of a coal-mine as a place at which the practical moral issues arise and are dealt with, as it were, at the coal-face, while the moral philosopher stands at the pit-head or in the operations room, trying to work out and systematize what is going on below.

What, then, do moral philosophers have to say about the 'logical geography' of morality? Philosophers, as we shall see, rarely agree about anything very much; argument and the opposition of conflicting positions lie at the heart of philosophical activity. As in any sphere of study, however, some views and conclusions are more commonly shared than others, and it is accordingly simplest to start from those features of morality over which there is least controversy, and proceed to the more contentious issues later. 'Least controversy', though, does not mean unanimity; philosophers delight in challenging established, orthodox viewpoints and theories, and this is exactly how the subject proceeds and develops. Nevertheless, in a book of this scope and length there is a limit to the number of alternative arguments which can be mentioned, and qualifications which can be made. The reader must not, then, assume at any point that a final, unchallengeable, 'right' answer has been given, for philosophy is not like that. Further reading, as suggested at the end of the book, will soon confirm this.

3.2 *The least controversial features of morality*

Some of these features have already been hinted at in connection with the 'moralistic argument' in Chapter 1. It was argued there that moral behaviour cannot be simply that which conforms to the dictates of some authority, because being moral cannot be equated with doing as one is told. This is not to say that people have to be disobedient and rebellious in order to qualify as moral agents, for it is of course possible to accord respect to an authority because one has judged that authority to be a source of reliable and wise instructions, but that is something different from blind conformity or obedience. (This point will be developed further in Chapter 5, section 1.) We cannot say that a person is engaged in the area of moral operations if he does what he does *merely* because he has been told to do it, without exercising some degree of independent judgement himself. Precisely what form of independent judgement is required here is highly debatable, as we shall find in the following two chapters, but to make any such judgement seems to bring in another generally agreed characteristic of moral behaviour – freedom of choice.

If I have no freedom to choose between alternative courses of action that are open to me, I surely cannot claim to be acting as a moral agent in doing whatever I do. Even if the consequences of my behaviour are universally agreed to be good, that behaviour cannot qualify as (descriptively) 'moral' if it was forced upon me and was thus unavoidable. A fanatical supporter of a famine relief organisation, for example, might compel me by means of drugs or hypnosis to write out a cheque to the charity for £1,000 (which could have the 'good' effect of alleviating much suffering), but my behaviour cannot fall within the 'moral' category, because it was not voluntarily undertaken. Or again, I cannot be acting as a moral agent if I accidentally bump into a blind man when crossing the road, and happen to knock him out of the way of an oncoming bus, even though a life may have been saved as a result of my clumsiness.

If we accept that voluntary choice and independent judgement, though difficult to define at times, seem to be two necessary features of morality, it follows that we cannot look merely at a person's outward behaviour to determine whether or not he is acting morally, because those features are often not observable. The last examples showed that my behaviour in writing a cheque to the charitable organisation, and in pushing a blind man out of danger, is not necessarily *moral* behaviour; it all depends on the circumstances in which I move my pen over the cheque, or cause the blind man to change direction. Particularly relevant, then, to whether my behaviour counts as 'moral' or 'non-moral' will be my *intentions, reasons* and *motives* (which is why *unintentional* behaviour must be classified as 'non-moral'). The same outward piece of behaviour may be interpreted in a wide variety of different ways, because of the wide variety of different reasons and motives which may lie behind it. A schoolgirl who offers to give up some of her free time to help tidy up the art room, for example, may be doing this for all sorts of reasons, some 'moral' and some 'non-moral': she may be feeling guilty for having left the room in a mess, or she may want to express her gratitude for the efforts of the art teacher, or she may have a crush on that art teacher, or she may be looking for an opportunity to steal some art materials. We cannot tell whether her action falls within the 'moral' category without knowing something of the reasons why she is acting in that way.

Philosophers may generally agree that certain reasons and intentions must lie behind moral behaviour, but they are by no means agreed as to what kind of reasons and intentions these must be. This is an important area of controversy which will be prominent in the following two chapters. Rather less controversial is the claim (which most non-philosophers would readily accept as a matter of common-sense) that, while having certain intentions and motives is a necessary part of being a moral agent, this is not sufficient in itself to constitute moral agency, for those intentions and motives must also lead one actually to perform the appropriate *action*. Morality is, by definition, a *practical* business, in that it is basically concerned with what ought to be *done*, and what it is right to *do*. Working out answers to moral problems and dilemmas in a purely theoretical way, as one solves a crossword clue, is not alone enough to qualify as 'being moral', if there is no consequent attempt made to act in accordance with one's conclusions. The precise relationship between moral judgement and moral action is a complex one, to which we shall return later, but it seems clear that morality must refer to how a person actually behaves, as well as to how he thinks.

This brief outline of some of the general features of morality which most philosophers would agree upon does not take us very far, largely because the features *are* so general, and consequently do not pick out anything very distinctive about the moral area. Also, they only offer *necessary* conditions of morality, not *sufficient* ones: that is, they are characteristics which a person's behaviour must necessarily have if it is to count as 'moral', but they do not give a full account of that behaviour which is sufficient to distinguish it from all 'non-moral' behaviour. Many actions are voluntary, intentional, and based upon independent judgement and reasons, without qualifying as 'moral'. A more specific description of the moral area is needed, and it is at this point that philosophers start to part company and the interesting disagreements develop.

Before reaching this point, however, we must pause to consider the implications of the account of morality which has so far been given. The features which have just been outlined, unspecific though they may be, nevertheless serve to eliminate certain types of behaviour from the 'moral' class. This means, of course, that if they cannot qualify under the descriptive definition of 'moral', they cannot proceed to the second round, as it were, as contenders for the accolade of (evaluative) moral *goodness*. This is well illustrated if we now look back at the range of claims made for children's moral goodness in examples (*a*)–(*k*) in the previous section, to see how they match up to these general moral requirements.

Clearly Jane (*a*), who always does as she is told, cannot count as a moral agent if she behaves as she does *simply* because she is told to do so, without attempting to exercise any independent judgement. John (*b*), who never argues or answers back, may well come into the same category; it all depends *why* he never argues or answers back. His docility might be the result of brain damage, or intellectual shortcomings, or a desire for a quiet life, or a fear of punishment, but none of these reasons could make John's behaviour moral. Likewise, the motives of Jean (*e*), who never misses a Sunday school class, of Jason (*f*), who has never been in trouble with the police, of Joan (*g*), who never skips her homework, and possibly even of Jill (*c*), who is always ready to help anyone in trouble, all need further elaboration before we can begin to decide whether they might fall within the moral area of operations, because overt behaviour alone cannot provide sufficient evidence. More information is needed in all these cases about the reasons which lie behind the child's behaviour and the context in which it occurs. Jean, for example, may be so unimaginative that she cannot think of anything else to do on a Sunday morning; Jason may be very good at escaping unseen from the scene of the crime, and leaving his accomplices to carry the can; Joan may do her homework every night with her father standing over her, strap in hand; while Jill may be the vicar's daughter, compelled to perform her charitable works to keep up appearances.

A different sort of question-mark hangs over James (*j*), who means well but often gets led astray. If he is led astray with monotonous regularity, how do we know that he really does mean well, and is not merely paying lip-service to his declared good intentions? And how often are we prepared to accept this disparity between his apparent intentions and his actual behaviour, before concluding that he is either so weak or so insincere that he cannot be said to be operating within the moral area at all? Similarly, it does not seem quite enough for Jim (*h*) just to feel upset when others are unhappy, or for Jonathan (*d*) to suffer pangs of guilt, if these feelings do not prompt them to do anything positive to remedy the situation.

Janine (*k*) avoids this criticism by always doing what she believes ought to be done, but we might want to know about the *sort* of things she believes ought to be done, and *why* she believes she ought to do them; a determination to paint her toenails exactly the right shade of purple, or to steal enough money to buy more fashionable clothes than all her friends, would not have much to do with the making of moral judgements. Finally, June (*i*) raises other problems by always doing what is right without having to think about it, for apart from the difficulty of determining how she knows what *is* 'right', how can 'not having to think about it' be reconciled with the moral requirement of exercising some degree of independent judgement? Can moral behaviour ever be purely habitual and non-reflective?

Much more could, of course, be said about all of these examples, and most of the queries raised about them will need to be expanded later. But even these first reflections serve to cast doubt upon whether many forms of children's behaviour that are often called 'good' can in fact qualify as *moral* behaviour at all, in the light of those generally agreed features of morality that we have so far uncovered.

Although our brief survey of these features has involved some preliminary spadework, a lot of ground remains to be cleared. A false impression may also have been given so far in this chapter, despite warnings to the contrary, that considerable unanimity exists among moral philosophers about the features of morality. It is now time, then, to examine more specific, conflicting accounts of those features, as this will serve the dual purpose of helping us to probe more deeply into what might be meant by children 'being good', and of illustrating the typical cut-and-thrust of philosophical disputation. Up to now references to individual philosophers or particular philosophical theories have been deliberately avoided, to enable the reader to get to grips directly with the basic problems with the minimum of complications and distraction. But we cannot now progress further without taking note of the radical disagreements which have divided moral philosophers, and which yield important practical implications for our investigation.

3.3 The form and content of morality

Philosophical attempts to define the moral area have tended to fall into one or other of two broad categories, concerned with what is usually labelled either the *form* or the *content* of morality. This distinction is a vital one for our purposes, and will be used as the basis for the following two chapters. Let us first consider an analogy which should help to make the distinction clear.

Suppose you were asked 'What is science all about?', or 'What is distinctive about science?', or 'What do you mean by "scientific"?'. You might give two different sorts of answer to those questions. On the one hand, you might say something like 'Science is about the physical structure of the world and the universe; what's distinctive about it is that it deals basically with how matter behaves – that's what scientific knowledge is all about.' Or, on the other hand, you might say: 'Science is a particular type of inquiry, which proceeds by setting up theories and hypotheses, and then testing them by practical experiments; this kind of method is what is distinctive of science and scientific work.'

Now, what the first answer is doing is to define 'scientific' in terms of the *content* of science – that is, the subject matter with which it typically deals, and which differs from the subject matter of, say, mathematics, which is concerned with such things as numbers and equations. But the second answer says nothing about content, for it offers a definition of 'scientific' in terms of the *form* of science – that is, the methods, procedures and reasoning it employs, which are again different from those of mathematics, to take the same example, because the methods of mathematics do not involve doing practical experiments to test hypotheses, but manipulating abstract symbols and making deductions from axioms. Incidentally, it is significant that these two definitions of science will produce differing interpretations of 'science *education*'. Those who define science in terms of its content will see the function of science education to be mainly one of passing on a particular subject matter and corpus of 'hard facts', comprising the discoveries and conclusions of scientists; whereas those who define science in terms of its form will have a conception of science education as the initiation of children into the scientific method and way of thinking.

This distinction between form and content is equally applicable to the area of morality. Some might say, on the one hand, that morality is to be defined in terms of its content, and that moral issues and questions are accordingly those which deal with a particular subject matter – for example, the pursuit of justice, or the consideration of other people's interests, or the promotion of human happiness and welfare. One would then be operating morally only when one was dealing with those issues and taking those factors into account in one's decisions and actions. But others might, on the other hand, try to define morality in terms of its form, which it might be claimed is reflected in the *way* in which moral judgements are made and moral conclusions reached – for example, in justifying one's particular actions by appealing to general, universal principles. In this case one would qualify as 'being moral' only when reasoning in that way. Again, as in the case of science, it is important to note that different *educational* implications follow from these two views of morality: the 'content' view will see moral education as being primarily concerned with passing on a definite subject matter in terms of specific rules and precepts about how to behave towards other people (e.g. the 'value transmission' approach), while the 'formal' view will emphasize certain ways of thinking and reasoning which children will need to acquire if they are to become 'morally educated' (e.g. the 'development of moral reasoning' approach).

The form-versus-content distinction, then, looks to be worth more detailed examination, if we wish to gain a clearer picture of the descriptive notions of morality and moral education. It is a much more complex distinction than has so far been suggested, however, because both viewpoints have been expressed in a number of different versions, with the result that there is as much dispute *within* each category as there is *between* them. Also, at times it is difficult to decide whether certain accounts of morality should be classified as 'formal' or 'content-based'. Nevertheless, a rough-and-ready classification in terms of form or content can be made of the most important philosophical positions, and in the following two chapters we shall consider in turn how adequate a picture of morality and moral education they offer, and what further issues they raise, before we try to come to any conclusions in the final chapter as to whether we really can teach children to be good.

4: What Is the Form of Morality and Moral Education?

There are several different ways in which philosophers have attempted to describe the form of morality. Some have concentrated upon the type of language in which moral statements are made, and have tried to work out the rules and structure of that language. Others have felt that moral language serves a particular function, and is used to achieve particular effects. Another school of thought sees something peculiarly distinctive in the act of making a moral choice. Yet a further approach seeks to analyse the precise method of reasoning by which we arrive at moral conclusions. In this chapter we shall look in some detail at these various theories and at the different pictures of moral education they suggest.

4.1 Prescriptivism

One of the best examples of a modern philosopher who has tried to present a 'formal' picture of morality is R. M. Hare, whose theory is usually labelled 'prescriptivism'. Hare provides an excellent starting-point for our survey, as he has also spelt out in some detail what he sees to be the implications of prescriptivism for the practical business of teaching children about morality.

The title of one of Hare's most influential books gives a good clue to his view of morality and its distinguishing features. The book is called *The Language of Morals* (Hare 1952), and the easiest way to get a grasp of the theory is to think of morality as exactly that – a *language*. Languages have their own form and structure; they are made up of words and concepts which are interconnected, and which can be used correctly or incorrectly; they have, to repeat a phrase introduced in the previous chapter, their own 'logical geography'. It is in these respects, according to Hare, that morality is essentially a language; which means that we can discover the meaning of 'moral' only by studying the *form of moral discourse*, that is, the language of morality.

What are the main characteristics of this language? What is its grammar? First, Hare claims that it has a special function, namely, *to guide conduct*, and it is this function which gives the theory of prescriptivism its name: 'The language of morals is one sort of prescriptive language' (Hare 1952, p. 1). For a judgement to count as a *moral* judgement (for instance, that it is right to respect one's parents), it must tell someone what to do (i.e. respect your parents). This means that the job of moral language is not primarily to tell us facts about the world, although moral judgements may incidentally convey some factual information and have what Hare calls a 'descriptive meaning': 'If a parson says of a girl that she is a good girl, we can form a shrewd idea of what description she is' (ibid., p. 146). The distinctive function of moral language, however, is to provide not *descriptive* answers about what is true or false (as scientific language tries to do, for example), but rather *prescriptive* answers about what to do.

Moral language, then, must be closely bound up with people's actions: 'If we were to ask of a person, "What are his moral principles?" the way in which we could be most sure of a true answer would be by studying what he *did* (ibid., p. 1, italics in original). Hare's argument here is a lengthy one, which can be briefly summarized as follows. Supposing I form the judgement 'I ought to respect my parents'; that can count as a *moral* judgement only if I address the appropriate prescription or imperative to myself ('Let me respect my parents'), and give my 'sincere assent' to that prescription; and giving my assent to the prescription requires that I *act* in accordance with it (by actually respecting my parents), provided that it is within my power to do so. The prescriptiveness of moral language thus emphasizes the practical nature of morality.

But Hare does not allow that *any* kind of prescription which leads to action in this way will qualify as a moral judgement, and this is where his second characteristic of moral language enters in. The moral judgement which I make, and the imperative which I assent to in one situation, I must also be prepared to make and assent to in *any similar situation*; for in Hare's terminology, moral judgements are *universal* as well as prescriptive. In effect, these two features operate together, as a simple example will illustrate. Tom complains that Jim is being unfair in refusing to let anyone else play with his new toy. That complaint, according to Hare's theory, involves the making of a *moral* judgement (as distinct from the mere expression of Tom's disappointment, or an attempt to get back at Jim) only if Tom is prepared to 'universalise his prescription' – that is, to accept that the same prescription ('share your toys with others') will apply to everyone else, *including himself*, who is placed in a similar position to that which Jim now occupies, as the owner of a new and coveted toy.

The combination of these two features of 'prescriptivity' and 'universality' produces for Hare a moral language of 'rigorous and austere simplicity'. In order to use that language correctly as a moral agent, one must first decide what actions one is prepared both to commit oneself to, and at the same time to 'accept as exemplifying a principle of action binding on anyone in like circumstances' (Hare 1963, p. 74). This account of morality has much in common with that of Immanuel Kant, who in the eighteenth century proposed a moral formula known as the 'categorical imperative', one version of which is expressed in similar terms to Hare's: 'Act only on that maxim which you can at the same time will to become a universal law' (Paton 1948, p. 29). Hare's account, however, is clearer and more straightforward for our present purposes of illustrating what a purely 'formal' picture of morality might look like.

Hare's work, to which the above outline cannot of course

do full justice, has attracted much attention and, like any important contribution to philosophy, has provoked a great deal of fruitful criticism and discussion. Much of this has centred on the two suggested characteristics of moral language, which many have thought to be not capable of doing the job that Hare claims they can do.

On the one hand, it has been pointed out that the two characteristics are shared by *other* forms of discourse as well as moral. In making practical judgements, for example, about how to build a garage, or aesthetic judgements about how to paint a picture, one is often issuing and accepting prescriptions which one would be prepared to universalize in the way that Hare describes, but that is surely not enough to make garage-building and picture-painting automatically into *moral* matters. All that Hare has done here, it can be argued, is to describe what it means to be *logically consistent* in considering courses of action, but that does not help us to demarcate the specifically *moral* area. This objection, then, denies that Hare's characteristics are *sufficient* conditions of moral language and moral judgement: they do not in themselves comprise a precise enough definition which rules out other kinds of language and judgement. Indeed, the mere universalizing of prescriptions seems to rule out practically nothing, as it is quite possible (in theory at least) to be willing to universalize the oddest of prescriptions (for example, that one ought always to wear red socks on Tuesdays, or that Pisceans ought never to grow parsnips), which it seems ridiculous to describe as 'moral'.

On the other hand, some critics have gone further than this by querying whether the two characteristics can even count as *necessary* conditions – that is, do all moral judgements *need* to possess these features? As far as prescriptivity is concerned, moral language does not seem to have only one function, namely, to guide conduct and tell people what to do. It is used, as Nowell-Smith points out, to play many different parts: 'to express tastes and preferences, to express decisions and choices, to criticise, grade, and evaluate, to advise, admonish, warn, persuade and dissuade, to praise, encourage and reprove, to promulgate and draw attention to rules; and doubtless for other purposes also' (1954, p. 98). In most of these cases moral language will be related to conduct in *some* way or other but that relationship is not as direct as Hare suggests.

If prescriptivity is a weak candidate as a necessary feature of all moral judgements, doubts have likewise been voiced about universality. Problems arise here over how exactly to apply and interpret the notion, and how to decide when one situation is 'similar' to another. No two situations can ever be identical in all respects, so in what respects do they have to be alike in order to count as 'similar', therefore requiring universalized treatment? However, the mere fact that universality is in practice a difficult requirement to interpret does not necessarily mean that Hare is wrong in seeing it as an essential element in morality.

A further difficulty about Hare's prescriptivism is that it appears to demand too close a connection between the making of moral judgements and their practical implementation. We noted in the previous chapter that morality is, in an important sense, a practical business, concerned with what ought to be *done*, and that if a person were consistently led astray from doing what he believed he ought to do, we would start to have reservations about his status as a moral agent. But Hare pushes this point to the extreme, in denying that we can be making moral judgements at all if we fail to act upon them. This seems to be ignoring what is surely another characteristic feature of morality, namely, that its demands are *difficult to live up to*. Supposing that a teacher believes that it is wrong to use sarcasm as a technique of control and punishment in the classroom; yet on occasions the temptation proves too great, when certain children particularly irritate him. His action makes him feel extremely guilty and remorseful, he is convinced that he has behaved wrongly, and resolves never to be sarcastic again in the classroom – though knowing in his heart of hearts that he may not be able to keep to this resolution in the heat of the moment. According to Hare, the teacher's judgements both before and after his sarcastic outbursts cannot properly count as 'moral' ones, because they were not acted upon; but surely this kind of situation is central to all people's moral experience (except in the case of saints, perhaps). In denying that sincere moral judgements can be made yet not acted upon at times, Hare is rejecting the possibility of *moral weakness* – that is, of failing to do that which one genuinely believes one ought to do (see Straughan 1982). However, this is to overlook something which seems as essential a feature of morality as Hare's own suggestions, and which is neatly expressed by Neil Cooper: 'Between principles and practice, ideal and fulfilment, there will in any normal morality be a gap – this gappiness is an essential feature of the moral life and is made manifest in the tension which may exist prior to action between principle and desire' (1971, p. 225).

In his later work Hare tries to elaborate his account of moral weakness, but this is not the place to consider his arguments in greater detail. Two features of this later work must be briefly noted, however. First, Hare places more emphasis upon what he claims is a third characteristic of morality – 'overridingness'. Moral principles and prescriptions override other kinds of principle and prescription (e.g. aesthetic, economic, legal, etc.) in the event of a clash or conflict, he maintains (1981, 3.6). This alleged characteristic will be considered further in 4.4, but at this point we can see that the phenomenon of moral weakness again suggests an obvious objection: as Thalberg neatly puts it, 'That is the very problem here: moral principles do not always win out. And it would be completely uninformative to be told only that moral reasons have greater *moral* authority' (1971, p. 241, italics in original). Secondly, Hare also places more emphasis upon moral 'intuitions', acquired from our upbringing and past experience: 'The intuitive level of moral thinking ... is an essential part of the whole structure' (1981, 2.5). This produces a more complex definition of morality, which Hare significantly admits 'brings us somewhat nearer the point of view of some who think of themselves as my opponents (who) wish to insist that no purely formal definition of "moral" can be given' (ibid., 3.8).

There are, then, major difficulties surrounding Hare's attempt to provide a purely 'formal' account of morality, but while they suggest that that account is not wholly adequate, they do not rob the theory of all its value. The emphasis upon the need for some kind of logical consistency, both in the making and in the implementation of moral judgements, is clearly important, even if overstated. The account also has interesting implications for our view of moral education, which Hare has himself been at pains to point out. This makes his theory a particularly good example for our purposes, as Hare stands almost alone among recent moral philosophers in being prepared to apply his analysis of morality directly to the practical business of teaching children. 'The question "How shall I bring up my children?"', he rightly observes, '...is one to the logic of which, since ancient times, few philosophers have given much attention' (1952, p. 74).

Hare's 'formal' account of morality, as might be expected, yields an equally 'formal' account of moral education, which is most clearly spelt out in an article entitled (significantly) 'Language and moral education' (1973). Form rather than content is what matters, he claims:

> I am convinced that if parents first, and then children, understood better the *formal* character of morality and of the moral concepts, there would be little need to bother, ultimately, about the content of our children's moral principles; for if the form is really and clearly understood, the content will look after itself.
>
> (ibid., p. 164, italics in original)

Taking the two proposed features of moral language, which we have already discussed (prescriptivity and universality), Hare tries to deduce from these a number of necessary requirements for moral education. The most important of these are as follows. First, if the function of moral judgements is to guide action, a moral educator must show that he is himself trying sincerely to live up to his principles and is not merely paying lip-service to them (ibid., p. 154). Secondly, if moral judgements are prescriptive rather than descriptive, children in being taught morality must be shown that moral judgements are not statements of fact to be learned, but choices of principles to be made, leading to the adoption of a particular way of life (ibid., p. 155). Thirdly, if moral judgements involve universalizing one's prescriptions, moral education must teach children how to put themselves into other people's shoes; and this in turn will require the ability to discern the feelings of others, and to predict the consequences of one's own actions upon them (ibid., p. 161). Fourthly and finally, if universality means that a moral agent cannot prefer his own interests to those of others, or view his own position as a privileged one, moral education must teach children to love their fellow men, and to treat their interests as of equal weight with their own (ibid., pp. 163–4).

In this way, Hare claims, children will be taught the form of morality. They will also no doubt incidentally pick up some of the *content* of their parents' and teachers' principles, which may or may not be rejected later; but what is important is that they should learn correctly how the language of morality works, and what it means to hold a moral principle, regardless of the precise content of that principle.

There are interesting similarities between the view of moral education which Hare arrives at and that proposed by other influential writers on the subject. In particular, the work of John Wilson (to which Hare in fact pays tribute in his article) underlines several of Hare's necessary requirements for moral education. Wilson has attempted in a number of books to identify the skills and dispositions which go to make up a morally educated person. These include the ability to translate one's principles into action, to have insight into other people's feelings, and to identify with others in such a way that their interests count as equal to one's own – all requirements which feature in Hare's list (Wilson, Williams and Sugarman 1967, pp. 192–4). Similarly, the Schools Council Project in Moral Education, described in Chapter 2, (2.4) places great weight upon predicting consequences and understanding other people's feelings.

But Hare's conclusions, however well they may fit in with other recent work on moral education, are based upon an analysis of morality which we have seen to be open to various criticisms. To what extent do these invalidate Hare's account of moral education? Clearly, if we cannot accept that prescriptivity and universality are sufficient to define all aspects of the complex area of morality, then we cannot rely upon them to provide a totally adequate foundation for moral education. Yet if we keep this probable inadequacy in mind, Hare's work can still be extremely useful, both in indicating some components which seem to be necessary in most aspects at least of moral education, and also in causing us to recognize some difficulties and omissions in his account of moral education which stem from his more general moral theory.

So, for example, even if moral language is not always prescriptive in Hare's sense, and even if there is a necessary 'gappiness' between moral principles and action which Hare underestimates, morality (and consequently moral education) must still, in an important sense, be a practical business, concerned with action as well as judgement; and Hare's first two educational implications are drawing attention to exactly that. Likewise in the case of his third implication, even if there are difficulties about deciding how and when to 'universalize a prescription' and what counts as a 'similar situation', some kind of sensitivity to the viewpoints and interests of others seems to be an undeniable element in most moral contexts, and therefore an obvious concern of moral education.

The fourth implication – that children should be taught to love their fellow men – raises deeper problems. Even if we feel inclined intuitively to agree with Hare that this is desirable (though likely to be difficult in practice), we must still ask precisely what this 'love' is, and whether it follows directly as a logical consequence of Hare's analysis of morality. 'Love' seems to be an ambiguous and misleading choice of term for what Hare appears to be meaning, as he identifies it immediately with treating the interests of others as of equal weight to one's own (1973, p. 164). So what kind of *affective* or *'feeling'* side to morality (if any) is Hare demanding here? It is quite possible to treat the interests of others as equal to one's own without feeling any affection, love, or even respect towards them. A colonial administrator, for example, might treat the interests of the local population as equal to his own, in dutifully ordering his province, applying (and obeying) its laws, collecting (and paying) its taxes, protecting individual rights, and so on; yet he might do all this in pursuit of efficiency, security, and his own promotion and reputation, while privately detesting and despising the people he is dealing with. Such a person is not preferring his own interests to those of others, but is he displaying 'love' in any sense, and can he be called a moral agent?

There seems to be a weakness in Hare's argument here, whichever way it is taken. On the one hand, his picture of morality and of the morally educated person is surely incomplete if only logical consistency and non-preferential treatment are demanded, as the above example suggests; the *spirit* in which one universalizes a prescription, and the *feelings* one has about the people involved, help to determine whether or not a moral action is taking place. But on the other hand, Hare's analysis of the language of morality attempts to show only that moral agents must *judge* and *act* in certain ways, not that they must have any particular *feelings* about their fellow men; indeed there is very little reference in that analysis to the emotional or the motivational aspects of morality. It is interesting, therefore, that Hare feels the need to introduce the notion of 'love' into his account of moral education, perhaps by way of compensation for the lack of any 'feeling' element in his earlier description of morality.

In his later work, where Hare lays more emphasis upon moral 'intuitions', a less 'formal' and more conventional picture of moral education emerges. 'A necessary part of moral education,' he argues, 'lies in the acquisition of moral attitudes – i.e. dispositions to have moral intuitions with a certain content and the associated moral feelings, and to act in accordance with them' (1981, 10.2). At another point he speaks with approval of 'implanting...a good set of principles plus the feelings that go with them' (ibid., 11.5). This seems far removed from Hare's earlier claim, quoted above, that if children understand the formal character of morality, there is 'little need to bother about the content of children's moral principles'. As seemed to be the case with Hare's general moral theory, these later conclusions about moral education appear to admit shortcomings in his earlier attempts to focus exclusively upon questions of form rather than content.

We have now looked in some detail at Hare's prescriptivist theory as a good example of an attempt to map out the form of morality and of moral education. The features and requirements it describes provide part of the necessary outline of moral behaviour, but do not give an adequate account of the many facets and dimensions of morality. Let us now consider rather more briefly some other 'formal' theories to see if they share this weakness with prescriptivism.

4.2 Emotivism

This theory pre-dated Hare's prescriptivism and has a certain amount in common with it. Emotivism has a long philosophical history behind it, but its fullest exposition is to be found in the work of Ayer and Stevenson (for example, Ayer 1936; Stevenson 1944). The main area of agreement with prescriptivism is a negative one – that moral judgements are not to be thought of as statements of fact, claiming 'descriptive meaning'. The distinguishing feature of moral language lies in what it expresses, for its characteristic function, according to emotivism, is to convey and influence emotional attitudes.

If, for example, I claim that it is wrong to perform painful experiments on live animals, what makes this a moral judgement is not that it is stating a truth, capable of some sort of verification, but that it is the equivalent of saying 'I don't approve of painful experiments on live animals; don't perform them or encourage them!' In other words, in making a moral judgement one is first expressing one's feelings in the form of approval or disapproval, and secondly trying to persuade others to share those feelings.

Morality, then, becomes a matter of exerting influence on others by expressing one's own sentiments. This makes moral utterances highly subjective, and thereby offers an explanation of why moral questions are so often marked by controversy and disagreement. My feeling that animal experiments are wrong may conflict with your feeling that they are right, in the same way that my fear of snakes may conflict with your love of them. Different emotional reactions can result from two people's experience of the same situation, and these differences cannot be 'resolved' objectively by discussion or an appeal to 'the facts' – though there is room for a certain amount of rational debate about what 'the facts' are (for example, how many animal experiments are actually performed each year?), as distinct from what emotional attitudes should be adopted towards them.

Philosophical criticisms of emotivism have followed the same general pattern as those of prescriptivism, by querying whether the so-called distinctive function of moral judgements is really as distinctive as is claimed. Clearly it is not only *moral* language that can be used to convey and influence emotional attitudes. Advertising, for example, also uses language for that purpose, yet few would accept that the script for a television commercial aimed at persuading us to drink more lager or smoke more cigars can, by any stretch of the imagination, be called a *moral* document. So the allegedly emotive function of moral language is certainly not sufficient to distinguish that language from other kinds of language.

Furthermore, as was suggested by some critics of prescriptivism, perhaps not even a *necessary* condition of moral language has been provided here. Does every possible use of moral language *have* to possess this emotive function, which is claimed to be distinctive of it? Opponents of emotivism have pointed out that moral judgements are often (perhaps even typically) made in a state of detached deliberation, where the aim is to lower, not raise, the emotional temperature. Cooper, who drew attention to the 'gappiness' existing between moral principles and practice, also speaks of the 'cool-hour' quality of moral principles, a suggestion which strikes at the heart of the emotivist position: 'a man's moral principles are those of his principles of action which in a cool hour he is least prepared to abandon belief in, however much he may be tempted to deviate from them in the heat of the moment' (1971, p. 197). *Conflict* then is possible, as we are all aware, between our moral judgements and our emotional responses, which means that the latter can hardly be a necessary characteristic of the former. Our experience of moral decision-making and moral conflict indicates that the problem is often to keep our emotions *in check*, when trying to work out the right thing to do (for instance, how to deal fairly with the irreconcilable claims of two people, one of whom you happen to like much more than the other). As P. H. Hirst puts it: 'Much moral debate is engaged in with the deliberate intent of removing the discussion from concern for emotional responses to a concern for making judgements on rational grounds' (1974, p. 38).

When we turn to look at the implications of emotivism for moral education, more of the theory's strengths and weaknesses become apparent. These educational implications have not been directly enunciated by emotivist philosophers as Hare has done for prescriptivism – which is hardly surprising, for on the emotivist interpretation of 'moral' moral *education* becomes a very dubious enterprise, as we shall shortly see. It is not too difficult, however, to detect traces of an implicit and unexamined kind of emotivism among those parents and teachers who are uneasy about the very idea of moral education, on the grounds that 'morality is just a matter of personal belief', and that 'if you feel it's right for you, then it's right'.

A more rigorous examination of these emotivist assumptions, however, reveals that the theory on which they are based implies a far less liberal view of the way in which children are to be introduced to the area of morality. If moral language (to which children will have to be exposed at some time in their upbringing and education) is to be distinguished by its supposed function of conveying and influencing emotional attitudes, it follows that in using moral language with children one is doing no more than persuading them to share the same attitudes as oneself, and to communicate these attitudes effectively to others. Granted there may be some scope for sorting out the facts of the matter (for instance, how much money is lost every year because of shop-lifting?), but once there is agreement on that, all that the teacher or parent can say about the *moral* issue of whether shop-lifting is wrong, or how shop-lifters ought to be dealt with, is to express his or her own feelings as forcefully as possible, with the intention of getting the children to share them.

Such a view of moral education does at least have the merit

of recognizing that moral judgements and decisions seem necessarily to contain some kind of 'feeling' element – a point which we saw was rather blurred in Hare's prescriptivist account of moral education. Moral issues are typically things that people *care* about and feel *committed* to doing something about, and it is important that children grasp these features of morality, and do not see moral discussion as a purely intellectual exercise. (Kohlberg's 'development of moral reasoning' approach to moral education, described in 2.5, has been criticized in this respect.) But the way in which this 'feeling' element is portrayed makes the emotivist picture of moral education hard to accept or even understand.

First, it is *subjective*, in the sense that the moral educator can only express his *own* feelings about the issue in question. Secondly, it is *non-rational*, in the sense that moral *discussion* or *debate*, involving any kind of objective appraisal, is strictly speaking impossible; all that can happen is the expression of various sets of feelings, which means that putting forward a moral argument is merely to make what R. S. Peters humorously calls 'a sophisticated sort of grunt' (1966, p. 109). And thirdly, it is *authoritarian*, in the sense that it entails manipulating the listener's feelings, and bringing psychological pressure to bear upon them in order to achieve conformity with the educator's feelings. Moral education thus becomes an exercise in propaganda and the techniques of persuasion, and the success of such teaching can only be measured in terms not of its promotion of understanding and insight, but of its effectiveness in producing the required emotional attitude and commitment; the Hitler Youth Movement comes to mind as an obvious example of the likely product of an emotivist approach to moral education.

The most fundamental weakness of emotivism, however, which is particularly well illustrated when the theory is translated into educational terms, is its oversimplified view of emotion itself. Emotivism maintains that our moral judgements stem directly from our feelings and emotions: we feel enraged, or disgusted, or attracted by something or someone, and that emotion *causes* us to make the moral judgement expressing our approval or disapproval. But this is to put the cart before the horse. The feelings of horror which we may experience on seeing a child brutally ill-treated does not *cause* our moral disapproval; it is rather because we judge the action to be morally wrong that we feel the horror and revulsion. We only experience emotional feelings as a result of already holding certain beliefs. A child, for example, must *know* quite a lot about natural history before he can feel afraid of poisonous toadstools or piranha fish; he does not *first* experience the emotion of fear and *then*, as a result, judge these things to be dangerous – except perhaps in the case of phobias and totally irrational fears, which are better described as pathological states than as emotions.

This confusion within emotivism is of special educational importance, for children cannot simply be *caused* to adopt ready-made emotional attitudes towards cruelty, unfairness, intolerance, and so on. Such moral feelings can only be derived from some objective understanding of events in the world (for example, that it hurts to have pins stuck in you). If emotions express our interpretations and understandings of the world, education has a central role to play in helping children to develop and critically revise these. We can, therefore, still retain some kind of 'feeling' element in our picture of morality without having to accept the emotivist version of moral education as a wholly subjective process of psychological manipulation and non-rational propaganda, unconnected with the development of knowledge and understanding. So although emotivism performs the service of alerting us to the importance of 'feeling' in some areas of morality and moral education, teaching children to be good need not be so uneducational an activity as emotivism implies.

4.3 Existentialism

The next example of a 'formal' theory of morality differs in several respects from the previous two. Existentialism, unlike prescriptivism and emotivism, is not a specifically *ethical* theory. Indeed, it is not a systematic, unified theory of any kind, as it encompasses a number of different strands, emphases and perspectives, often with only the loosest of links existing between them. The point of including existentialism in this survey is not, therefore, to provide any general overview of the philosophical trends and attitudes which it represents, nor to delve too deeply into the frequently obscure language and ideas in which it has been expressed. Our focus of attention here will be confined to the view of morality and moral decision-making which is put forward by one leading existentialist philosopher, Jean-Paul Sartre, particularly in his lecture *Existentialism and Humanism* (1973); for Sartre there makes a claim which certainly seems to entitle him to inclusion in this chapter: 'although the content of morality is variable, a certain form of this morality is universal' (p. 52).

It is not easy to summarize Sartre's argument without becoming entangled in the complexities of his more general philosophic stance, but basically his position is that an action is 'moral' only if it is *freely chosen and performed*. 'Man is nothing else but that which he makes himself', he claims (ibid., p. 28), which means that man's power of *choice* is all-important: 'To choose between this or that is at the same time to affirm the value of that which is chosen; for we are unable ever to choose the worse' (ibid., p. 29). Furthermore, in making this affirmation of value through our choices, we can appeal to no external authority or principle by way of justification: 'we have neither behind us, nor before us in a luminous realm of values, any means of justification or excuse. We are left alone, without excuse' (ibid., p. 34).

To illustrate this somewhat puzzling notion of what has been labelled 'criterion-less choice', Sartre quote a real-life example, which has since been extensively discussed by philosophers. A pupil of Sartre's during the Second World War was living alone with his mother, who was estranged from her husband and had already lost her only other son in action. The remaining son was the mother's only consolation, but he now had to make a choice between staying with his mother and joining the Free French Forces in England. Should he join the fight against Nazi Germany, or remain at home to support his mother? Sartre describes the young man facing these two alternatives, 'the one concrete, immediate, but directed towards only one individual; and the other an action addressed to an end infinitely greater, a national collectivity, but for that very reason ambiguous', and hesitating between two kinds of morality, 'on the one side the morality of sympathy, or personal devotion and, on the other side, a morality of wider scope but of more debatable validity' (ibid., pp. 35–6).

The point of this example, Sartre maintains, is that it shows that there is nothing – no moral authority, doctrine, or principle – that can help the son to make his moral choice. Nothing is solved by appealing to considerations of love, or charity, or self-denial, or respect for others, because these cannot adjudicate between the rival claims of his mother and his fellow countrymen by establishing that one has priority over the other: 'principles that are too abstract break down when we come to defining action' (ibid., p. 52). All that we can do as moral agents, concludes Sartre, is to 'trust in our instincts' (p. 36); the young man was 'obliged to invent the law for himself' (p. 49). Even here we cannot rely for guidance upon the strength of our feelings, however, for these cannot be known in advance of our performing the action that we have chosen. The form of morality for Sartre, then, is distinctive in that moral decisions have always to be 'invented' by the agent, and 'the one thing that counts is to know whether the invention is made in the name of freedom' (p. 53).

Sartre's emphasis upon free choice and independent judgement is not in itself particularly controversial, for as we saw in Chapter 3 most moral philosophers would agree that these features are necessary conditions of any moral decision or action. The reason why Sartre's account has attracted a great deal of philosophical interest and criticism is that he appears to make these features *sufficient* conditions of moral judgement and behaviour. No further tests can be applied to determine the moral nature of a decision, once it is established that it was 'freely chosen' or 'freely invented'; any other factor, such as the support of reasoned argument or an appeal to more general principles, is apparently irrelevant.

Leaving aside the problem of how precisely to define or

recognize this 'free choice', the most obvious charge to be levelled against Sartre's view of morality is that it is far too undemanding. Does the term 'moral' really signify nothing more than 'freely chosen'? Can any decision, however trivial, irrational, unconsidered, or unfeeling, count as a moral one, provided that this single requirement is satisfied? Some critics have suggested in this connection that Sartre's key example of the French student does not clinch his argument in the way that he claims. Would Sartre, for instance, have deemed 'moral' *any* course of action that the son decided on 'freely', such as slowly poisoning his mother with arsenic perhaps, in order that he might invest the inherited family fortunes in vintage claret? It is highly significant that Sartre describes the situation in a way which drastically *limits* the options open to the son: 'But he, at this moment, had the choice between going to England to join the Free French Forces or of staying near his mother and helping her to live' (ibid., p. 35). But why these *particular* options, if all that was required of the son as a moral agent was that he should 'trust in his instincts' and 'invent the law for himself'? Could not his instincts have led him into administering the arsenic? Might not his moral dilemma have been over how best to get hold of the poison, or whether to spend his mother's nest-egg on wine or on women, rather than over the issue which Sartre describes? Such questions sound farcical because we simply do not use 'moral' in that way; but Sartre's account cannot rule out such usages, which strongly suggests that there is something wrong with it.

By probing Sartre's example in this way, we soon realize that he is in fact operating with a far tighter definition of 'moral' than he is prepared to admit. He can put his example forward *as* a comprehensible example of a moral dilemma only if he sees in it, and expects us to see in it, features which are commonly thought to characterize moral issues and to constitute moral problems – in this case, the conflict of *duties* generated by one's feelings of *obligation* to further the *welfare* of various individuals and groups. The young man is seen by Sartre and by us as a *moral* agent making a *moral* choice not merely because he is acting freely, but because he is considering certain options rather than others, is troubled by certain problems rather than others, feels that certain consequences matter rather than others, and believes that certain factors are relevant to his decision rather than others. So it transpires that Sartre's example presupposes precisely what he wants to deny – a substantial framework of moral assumptions and principles, which require far more of a moral decision than that it is just 'freely chosen'.

At times Sartre does actually hint at what these additional principles might be. In particular, he comes very close in places to accepting Hare's view about the universality of moral judgements: 'When we say that man chooses himself, we do mean that every one of us must choose himself: but by that we also mean that in choosing for himself he chooses for all men' (ibid., p. 29). So, 'if I decide to marry and have children . . . I am thereby committing not only myself, but humanity as a whole, to the practice of monogamy' (p. 30). Hare interprets this as indicating that 'Sartre himself is as much of a universalist as I am, in the sense in which I am' (1963, p. 38). Nevertheless, it is difficult to see how Sartre can reconcile his emphasis upon free, criterion-less choice with this apparent support of the specific principle of universality, without severely restricting that choice and thereby rendering his description of moral decision-making somewhat incoherent.

The educational implications of Sartre's account, as in the case of prescriptivism and emotivism, highlight the theory's strengths and weaknesses. The importance of learning to use one's own independent judgement in making moral decisions, instead of relying wholly upon some external authority, is one of our recurrent themes in this book, and Sartre's emphasis upon this feature of morality encourages us to think critically about how it might be interpreted in the context of moral education. By implication, he rejects the idea of *teaching* children to be good, by thrusting upon the children themselves responsibility for their choices and actions, and by requiring them to 'invent the law' for themselves in order to qualify as moral agents. This conception of moral education has obvious affinities with those of some 'progressive' educators, such as A.S. Neill, who believe that children can only develop morally by exercising their freedom, without the attempted imposition of adults' moral values and assumptions. 'Freedom is necessary for the child because only under freedom can he grow in his natural way – the good way', proclaims Neill (1968, p. 108). And again: 'The external imposition on children of adult conceptions and values is a great sin against childhood ... The child should not do anything until he comes to the opinion – his own opinion – that it should be done' (ibid., pp. 110–11).

The question then arises, however, as to how children (and in particular young children) *learn* to reach such opinions and grow in Neill's 'natural, good way', or as Sartre would put it, to trust in their instincts and invent the law for themselves. How can this learning – if it is to be any kind of *moral* learning that is – take place without a great deal of guidance, teaching, demonstration and explanation, which must in turn depend upon the child's acceptance of some external authorities, rules and principles? If, for example, Johnny develops a liking (perhaps 'natural' and 'instinctual') for kicking his little sister in order to hear her cry, he can only be brought to see that this is a *moral* matter, capable of *moral* interpretation and formulation, in which *moral* responsibility can be exercised, by means of various authoritative procedures designed to modify his beliefs, attitudes and actions; and these will probably include the explanation, justification and, if necessary, imposition of certain simple moral rules about the right and wrong ways of treating little sisters.

These early stages of moral education raise awkward problems for Sartre, because his view of morality seems to make a total mystery of how anyone could ever start to *become* a moral agent, and accordingly of how children could ever learn to be good. If we really are, as Sartre claims, 'left alone' with no authorities, doctrines, or principles to help us develop any moral awareness, how can we ever begin to understand moral language and moral concepts, or begin to grow into responsible moral agents who have only to 'trust in our instincts'? Our instincts and feelings are informed and shaped by the upbringing we have had and the language through which we have learned to express and interpret our experience; so if they are to become *moral* instincts and feelings, they will need to have been *morally* informed by the rules and values we learn during our childhood. Otherwise there seems no reason why our instincts should be thought to have anything more to do with morality than have the instincts of a cuckoo or a vulture.

Thinking about the early stages of children's moral development and learning underlines the extent to which Sartre's existentialist account of morality relies upon a pre-existing framework of rules, principles and assumptions, which he tries to deny. Teaching children to be good, according to Sartre's definition of morality, would be to encourage them to choose and act freely, without offering any of the preliminary guidance and teaching which seems on reflection to be necessary in order to initiate the young into the realm of morality.

4.4 Principle application

The fourth and final sample of a 'formal' picture of morality encompasses a variety of viewpoints which cannot be directly identified with the theories of any one philosopher or school of philosophy, but which stem from arguments developed by Aristotle over 2,000 years ago. The underlying theme of this approach finds expression in a term whose everyday meaning needs no philosophical expertise to understand – 'a man of principle'. We speak of men (and women) of principle when we wish to draw attention to their behaviour as *moral* agents, the implication being that 'having principles' is intimately connected in some way with being moral.

This connection, many philosophers have felt, depends upon the common factor of *generality* which is shared by both principles and morality. As far as principles are concerned, they are general by definition, in that they are intended to guide conduct not by issuing specific, unequivocal instructions to a person faced with making a moral decision, but by offering a more abstract set of considerations and directives which can be appealed to in order to *justify* a particular choice (for example, the general principle of truth-telling might be appealed to by a doctor, when faced with the particular dilemma of whether or not to break some bad news to a certain patient). Equally, morality itself is often thought to contain a necessarily general component, in the sense that it suggests a rational, non-arbitrary method of determining what ought to be done: 'a central theme of moral philosophy is the belief that the moral sphere is not totally local, private or unique, but rather has certain general characteristics' (Chazan and Soltis 1975, p. 9). In other words, the doctor's decision about what to tell the patient, in so far as it is a *moral* decision, cannot be made simply on the basis of how he happens to be feeling that day, or how much he happens to like or dislike the patient, or whether the coin he tosses happens to come down heads or tails.

Already we can see that such an emphasis upon the role played by general principles in the field of morality would have much in common with Hare's prescriptivism but not with emotivism or existentialism. Hare's theory could in fact be seen as one version of principle application, and his requirement of universality for all moral principles is one way in which the generality of morality could be interpreted – that is, that a moral judgement made in one situation must be *generally applicable* to other similar situations. Emotivists on the other hand would be quite happy to accept that moral judgements, as expressions of a person's emotional attitudes, could be 'local, private or unique'; while Sartre's existentialist position, though appearing somewhat inconsistently to support Hare's demand for universality, is predominantly hostile to the idea that moral decisions can be made and justified by appealing to external principles.

Nevertheless, philosophers from the time of Aristotle have argued with a fair degree of unanimity that principles are basic to the very idea of morality. This apparent agreement, however, soon starts to break down when we look in more detail at the conflicting claims which have been put forward, first for the moral *superiority* or *priority* of certain principles over others, and secondly for the distinctive ways in which principles operate in moral reasoning. The former dispute can be left aside until the next chapter, as it is really concerned with the possible *content* of morality rather than its form (e.g. is truth-telling a more 'central' moral principle than consideration for others' feelings?) – though, as we shall shortly discover, it is very difficult to avoid the question of content when discussing moral principles. The latter dispute, however, directly refers to the *method* of principle application as a 'formal' feature of morality, and so demands our immediate attention.

Precisely how are principles related to moral judgements and moral actions? The traditional answer, first offered by Aristotle, is that a process of logical deduction is required, which takes the form of a 'practical syllogism' (1955, bk 7, ch. 3). According to this view, there are three elements in moral reasoning and decision-making: first, a general principle which states that a broad category of behaviour is right or wrong (for instance, it is wrong to break promises); secondly, the recognition that a particular situation falls within that category, and so is governed by the principle (for instance, I made a promise when I undertook to drive my neighbour to the doctor's surgery this evening); and thirdly, the conclusion that a particular action ought or ought not to be done (e.g. I ought to drive my neighbour to the surgery). Moral mistakes, then, come to be made because of some flaw in reasoning or understanding: either the original principle is not properly grasped, or the particular situation is not recognized as an instance to which the principle applies, or the logical conclusion is not drawn.

This Aristotelean description of principle application certainly does justice to the rational features of morality, which we saw to be largely ignored by emotivism and existentialism. In particular, it offers some rules and procedures for distinguishing good from bad moral reasoning, just as we can judge the validity of scientific, or mathematical, or historical conclusions. Yet, as with the previous three theories in this chapter, principle application can hardly claim to present a wholly adequate account of the form of morality.

In the first place, the objection which was levelled against Hare's prescriptivist theory applies with even greater force here. Does *any* general principle from which logical deductions can be made according to the 'practical syllogism' exemplify distinctively *moral* reasoning? There are surely a vast number of principles (for example, of karate or astrology or pornographic photography), the implementation of which has nothing to do with morality, however rational the process may be. The 'practical syllogism' can yield practical conclusions derived from these kinds of principle just as logically as it can from the principles of truth-telling and promise-keeping, so the reasoning procedure in itself does not seem to pick out anything that is distinctively 'moral'. Again we are faced with a set of conditions which may perhaps qualify as necessary for moral reasoning, but which cannot be sufficient. Even if the further move is made, as it has been by Hare and other philosophers (for example, Nowell-Smith 1954, pp. 307–8), of arguing that moral principles are those which are 'dominant' or 'over-riding' for a person, the same problem remains, for it is, in theory, quite possible to hold *any* principles as being 'dominant' or 'over-riding', in the sense of their being given priority by that person and acted upon: the principle of personal privacy may be 'dominant' for me, and the logical deductions I draw from it may lead me to spend all of my free time patrolling the boundaries of my garden with a shot-gun, but this is hardly an obvious example of *moral* reasoning or behaviour.

A second objection to principle application is that it leaves out of its picture of morality a whole area of deliberation which appears to be central to our moral experience. Principles cannot provide direct solutions to moral problems, partly because the principles themselves can and often do *conflict*; and the balancing of conflicting principles is itself a fundamentally moral activity, about which the theory, in so far as it merely describes a form of reasoning from principle to conclusion, can have nothing to say. The doctor who has to decide whether or not to break the bad news to his patient may not subscribe only to the principle of truth-telling, but also to that of preventing unnecessary suffering. Logical deduction alone can do nothing to resolve this dilemma, yet it is undeniably a *moral* dilemma requiring a *moral* decision. The theory fails, then, to describe how we weigh one principle against another, or even how we come to arrive at certain principles rather than others in the first place, both of which procedures must involve important moral choices.

Thirdly, even if there is no clash of principles, difficulties frequently arise over their interpretation and implementation, but the theory of principle application again ignores this typically moral problem. The doctor, faced with his unsuspecting patient, may wish to adhere to the principle of considering other people's feelings and interests, but how does this principle help him to reach a conclusion about what he ought to do? Many different courses of action could be justified by appealing to this general principle – for example, telling the patient the truth or telling him lies, informing the patient's family or keeping them in ignorance, prescribing drugs which will lessen his pain but shorten his life or withholding them, and so on. The form of reasoning described in the 'practical syllogism' gives no indication as to how the moral problem of interpreting such principles is to be approached – a point which Sartre quite rightly emphasizes, as we have seen: 'principles that are too abstract break down when we come to defining action' (1973, p. 52).

Fourthly and finally, it is by no means always self-evident that a particular situation *does* fall under a certain principle, and it is often not logical reasoning but some sort of moral sensitivity and imagination that is needed to recognize this. We may, for instance, accept the principle that stealing the property of others is wrong, yet fail to see that tax evasion, fiddling the social security, or not paying one's bus fare could be counted as instances of what the principle is condemning. Supermarkets nowadays show that they appreciate this point by displaying notices informing us 'Shop-lifting is stealing', which are presumably aimed, not at improving their customers' logical reasoning, but at alerting their awareness and sensitizing their imaginations – a job which has to be done *before* principles can be actually applied and conclusions drawn.

The application of principles, then, represents only one part of morality, however important that part may be. It is still instructive, however, as in the three preceding sections, to consider some of the implications for moral education which would follow from this account of morality, and to see what further strengths and weaknesses in that account they bring to light.

Principle application, unlike emotivism and existentialism, does at least appear at first sight to provide something substantive that can actually be *taught* to children – something that they can get right or wrong, and improve at. Moral issues become public matters, as scientific problems or historical puzzles are, which can be discussed rationally, instead of being the exclusive preserve of private sentiments or free choices.

But what exactly would children have to be taught, according to this view of morality, in order to become morally educated? Presumably they would need to learn a *method* by which principles can be applied to particular situations, and deductions drawn about what ought to be done; but when described in these terms, the whole enterprise acquires an air of unreality. How could one ever teach a method of this kind without also teaching a particular set of principles upon which the method is to be practised? To attempt this would be the equivalent of trying to teach children how to reason scientifically without supplying them with any basis of scientific knowledge to work from. And once we start teaching them to make deductions from *certain* principles rather than others, we are implying that a distinctive *content* as well as a distinctive form of morality can be identified, and we will then need a further argument to justify the selection of those moral principles. It is difficult to see, therefore, how a 'content-free' programme of moral education, directed solely towards teaching the so-called form of moral reasoning, could ever get off the ground.

This suggests a further practical difficulty. Even if principle application is acceptable as at least a partial account of the structure of moral reasoning, it does not follow that the formal deductions which it describes must be the method by which children learn to think morally. In retrospect, we may be able to analyse a moral action which we took in terms of Aristotle's 'practical syllogism', but that does not mean that we necessarily went through all the stages of that syllogism at the time, in the order that Aristotle describes. On many occasions there simply is not time consciously to work through this chain of reasoning (a man who hesitates on the canal bank, muttering 'I must see what the practical syllogism tells me to do here', while a child drowns in front of him, is hardly behaving morally); while on other occasions we may not have a clear-cut principle to apply at the beginning, but by grappling with the situation and visualizing alternative courses of action, we may *as a result of our decision* formulate a particular principle at the end rather than at the start of our moral deliberations. Similarly, children usually come to learn and accept principles through their practical experience of situations which are interpreted for them into moral language; for example, a child will grasp the principle of fairness, not by learning it first and then applying it, but by encountering instances of fair and unfair treatment, and by learning to translate these events into moral terms. Principles cannot then 'come first' in moral learning, because they can have no meaning or application unless they are *derived from* a child's experience of actual situations.

Older children might, however, be taught to 'apply principles' in accordance with the 'practical syllogism', but another weakness then becomes apparent, for what exactly does the 'conclusion' which is deduced from the principle consist of? Is it merely an intellectual judgement (that I ought to visit my grandmother this afternoon), or is it the action itself (of actually visiting my grandmother)? Aristotle and his numerous commentators are unclear on this point, but there do seem to be difficulties in the notion of 'deducing an action' directly from a chain of reasoning, because actions are normally thought of as the results of decisions and intentions rather than of logical deductions. If, then, the end-product of principle application is merely a moral *judgement* (which seems the most reasonable interpretation), it cannot provide an adequate model for moral education because, as we have already noted, behaviour is as important in morality as is reasoning. Placing too much emphasis upon principle application, therefore, in moral education could lead to an over-intellectualized approach, which concentrates upon the development of moral thinking rather than the performance of moral actions.

Despite these objections to the idea of a 'content-free' method of principle application as the basis of moral education, a number of influential writers have argued in various ways that the learning and application of principles is central to children's moral development. R. S. Peters, for example, as we shall see in the next chapter, distinguishes between different levels of rules and principles, and considers the different roles that these might play in moral education (1974). John Wilson claims that one of the defining characteristics of a morally educated person is that he is able to formulate rationally rules and principles to which he commits himself (Wilson, Williams and Sugarman 1967, p. 193). Lawrence Kohlberg, as we saw in Chapter 2 (2.5), attempts to describe a sequence of stages through which we all must pass in the process of our moral development, and defines the highest stage of moral reasoning in terms of following self-chosen ethical principles (1976, p. 35).

It is significant, however, that each of these writers in effect rejects, either explicitly or implicitly, a purely 'formal', 'content-free' view of morality and moral education, by referring to moral principles of a particular kind, arising in particular contexts and involving particular considerations. Thus, Peters argues for a specific set of fundamental moral principles (see 5.4 below); Wilson requires that the principles which his morally educated person formulates must be based upon identification with other people's feelings and interests; while Kohlberg virtually equates the 'self-chosen ethical principles' which mark his highest stage of moral development with the single principle of *justice* (1970). It seems fairly safe to conclude, therefore, that although principles appear in some way to play a necessary part in both morality and moral education, a purely 'formal' description of such principles remains incomplete, and we should accordingly perhaps follow the lead of Peters, Wilson and Kohlberg by probing more deeply into the question of content, and trying to determine what the precise ingredients of moral principles might be.

This chapter has been inconclusive in the sense that no wholly adequate theory has emerged, sufficient in itself to define the whole moral area, and thereby to map out the territory of moral education. A number of features has been found, however, which point to characteristics which are either necessary to the meaning of morality, or at least typical of most, if not all, the ways in which we use the descriptive term 'moral'. Prescriptivism, for example, has underlined the requirements of logical consistency; emotivism has drawn attention to some kind of 'feeling' component; existentialism has emphasized independent judgement; while principle application has stressed the generality and rationality that seem to underlie morality. These features, when added to those already outlined in Chapter 3, start to pick out some at least of morality's contours.

Examining the implications for moral education of these four accounts has provided further insight, first into the strengths and weaknesses of each theory, and secondly into the nature of the 'subject' with which moral education is concerned. Asking questions about how we can teach children to be good can in this way clarify our ideas about what 'being good' actually means. Hare is quite right, then, when he claims that 'many of the dark places of ethics become clearer' when we ask the question 'How shall I bring up my children?' (1952, p. 75).

These purely 'formal' descriptions of morality, however, have in themselves yielded fairly insubstantial and at times incoherent conclusions for the practical business of moral education, and the reason for this has often been simply because they *are* attempting to be 'formal' and 'content-free'. We must now turn, therefore, to an alternative set of approaches, which try to demarcate the moral area by means of its content, and see whether they offer a more tangible basis for teaching children to be good.

5: What Is the Content of Morality and Moral Education?

The question of content is best tackled by first re-focusing upon the subject of moral rules and principles. This is because any attempt to define morality and moral education by means of their content will have to spell out what that content is in terms of particular rules or principles, for that is the way in which the subject matter of morality is expressed. If, for example, one wants to argue that morality is essentially concerned with justice, or charity, or chastity, or honesty, or truthfulness, in each case one is referring to a rule or principle whose function is to guide conduct and to help resolve problems about what ought to be done. Similarly, any 'content-based' approach to moral education will aim at teaching a certain set of rules and principles to children. (The distinction between rules and principles will be further elaborated in this chapter and the next, but for the moment we can simply take rules to indicate the more concrete, specific prescriptions – 'You should give your seat up to old ladies in buses', and principles the more abstract, generalized ones – 'One should pay equal consideration to the interests of all people'.)

It is clearly possible to claim that any of a large number of rules and principles, or sets of rules and principles, is distinctive and definitive of morality, and it would be a formidable task to examine all of the conceivable candidates in turn. A more practicable strategy is to categorize these 'content-based' accounts under a few broad headings, not according to the particular rules and principles being proposed, but according to the *source* from which they are derived and the kind of *justification* on which they depend. All moral rules and principles must be grounded in some explicit or implicit justification, even at the level of 'Don't stamp in puddles because Mummy says so!' So by looking at some of the ways in which 'content-based' definitions of morality try to establish what moral rules and principles must be concerned with, we shall be able first to survey a fair sample of particular rules and principles which have been proposed, and secondly to see how the various systems of justification can produce different conceptions of moral education.

5.1 Appeals to authority

This category, as we have already seen in Chapters 1 and 3, is an important one, for although no modern philosopher is likely to argue that the content of morality can be sufficiently described in terms of rules and principles which derive their validity purely from an appeal to some form of external authority, many 'common-sense' views of morality are based precisely on that assumption. In many people's minds, for example, moral principles are identified and equated with particular rules about sexual behaviour, and these rules may often (though not always) depend for their supposed justification upon the authoritative pronouncements of parents, teachers, or the church. To be moral, then, on this interpretation is simply to live in accordance with certain sexual rules ('No sex before or outside marriage'), which are validated by appeals to authority ('That's what my father told me' or 'That's what the Bible says').

This is not, of course, the only kind of justification that could be offered for such rules; one might appeal to other 'non-authoritative' considerations, like personal satisfaction, social cohesion, the preservation of the family unit, or the prevention of sexually transmitted diseases. Nor should it be assumed that only sexual rules may be identified with morality in this way; the principles of paying one's way, working one's hardest, respecting one's elders and betters and not having ideas above one's station are further examples of rules that serve to define 'morality' for some people. Nor again is it only 'traditional', 'conservative' values of the kind so far mentioned which may provide the content of an authority-centred morality, for the moral life might equally be held by some people to be that which accords with the principles of self-sufficiency, consciousness-raising, vegetarianism and organic gardening, as prescribed by the edicts of the latest guru or commune-leader.

A very wide range of moral content, therefore, could be derived from appeals to authority, though it is more likely to take the form of relatively clear-cut, concrete rules of behaviour, than of more generalized, abstract principles which call for a greater degree of personal interpretation and understanding, because the main point of issuing authoritative pronouncements is to rule out the possibility of independent judgement. Thus, 'I always consider other people's interests because Mum told me to' sounds odd in a way in which 'I always say no to married men because Mum told me to' does not.

Attempts to define the content of morality in this way, however, are doomed to failure for reasons which have already been given. In Chapter 1 it was pointed out that nothing can ever become morally right because someone says that it is so, and that obedience to an authority is, strictly speaking, irrelevant to the business of moral decision-making; while at various points in Chapters 3 and 4 we have noted that exercising some degree of free choice and independent judgement seems to be a necessary part of what it means to be a moral agent.

Yet there is a great danger of drawing false conclusions from these well-established points and finishing up in a position close to Sartre's, where one must 'invent' morality for oneself without the aid or influence of any external guidance. The arguments against authority-based conceptions of morality only hold in those (perhaps relatively uncommon) cases where the appeal is made exclusively to the mere existence of the authority in question, and where one's 'moral' beliefs are, as Kurt Baier puts it, simply taken from those one has been taught blindly to revere (1973, p. 108). So if I hold that it is wrong to drink or smoke because my father says so, and if it really is the fact alone that he does say so to which I am appealing, then my belief is of an arbitrary kind which cannot count as a moral judgement. But if I hold that it is wrong to drink or smoke because my father has pointed out and explained to me the dangers and problems which these activities may create, or because I admire and value the abstemious lifestyle which my father exhibits, then my belief does not rest upon the mere fact of his making a pronouncement, but upon other considerations to which he has drawn my attention and which I have independently evaluated for myself.

The notion of 'moral authority', then, is not necessarily a self-contradictory one, for unless we are to accept Sartre's picture of the totally isolated, self-sufficient moral agent, we must allow that we do in practice value the moral advice and guidance of some people more highly than others, not just 'because they say it's right', but because they may have previously directed our attention to the moral aspects of situations in a way which we have found illuminating. We judge them to have a good track record as moral counsellors, and in so doing we are ourselves making a moral appraisal of their qualifications. Baier illustrates this point with the example of an Irish peasant accepting the authoritative advice of his priest about divorce and birth control: 'the peasant has independence of judgement so long as he accepts the priest's judgement only because he lacks the necessary expertise in these matters himself, believes (perhaps on good grounds) that the priest has it, and trusts the priest as well as his judgement' (ibid., p. 109). Similarly, we might accept the Sermon on the Mount as being morally authoritative, not merely 'because it was Jesus talking', but because of *our* assessment of the Sermon's moral quality or of Jesus as a reliable moral guide. Although nothing can ever be made morally right, therefore, by someone saying that it is so, that does not prevent us from judging as moral agents that there are good reasons for paying heed to the moral guidance of some authorities.

These suggestions gain further confirmation when we turn to look at the kind of approach to moral education implied in a view of morality which derives its distinctive content from appeals to authority. Clearly, extreme versions of this view which rely solely on the *fact* that such-and-such an authority exists and pronounces will result in rigid codes of conduct being laid down for children to follow unquestioningly, often reinforced by punishments to be inflicted for breaches of the authority's rules – though whether such a process can properly be allowed the title of 'moral education' (as distinct from 'training', 'conditioning', or 'indoctrination') is questionable. The content of morality in such cases may be defined as rules concerning, for instance, orderly behaviour, neatness, cleanliness, politeness and truthfulness, though we noted earlier in this section that 'progressive' values may have just as authoritative a source as 'traditional' ones. However, the highest moral accolade will probably be reserved for respect for authority itself, as a general rule or principle, because it is only through adherence to that precept that such a system can be maintained; conversely, critical questioning will normally be seen as an educational and moral *vice* rather than virtue, as it poses a threat to the status and reputation of the authority.

This description of 'moral education' sounds decidedly Dickensian, yet there must be few teachers or parents who can deny ever having responded to a child's 'Why...?' with that most economical of answers, 'Because I say so!' And indeed, is this answer *always* to be deplored? Elaborate, reasoned explanation and justification is sometimes inappropriate in the hurly-burly of a classroom or playground or family riot, and an emphatic reference to the teacher's or parent's role as an authority may on such occasions be the most effective (or the only) way of supporting a moral directive. Yet although this kind of procedure may occasionally be justifiable, the fact remains that a system of control which tries to transmit a particular code of conduct to children, simply by pointing to the fact that that code is prescribed by some authority, cannot claim to be doing anything that can be called either moral or educational.

Getting children to be obedient is not the same as teaching them to be good.

A further problem now arises, however, about the *learning* of moral rules and principles. Despite the obvious objections we have noted to a wholly authority-based view of morality and moral education, it appears that young children do as a matter of fact see the dictates of authority as a sufficient and valid form of moral justification. Some of Piaget's work, for example (1932), suggests that authoritative rules are thought by young children to possess a sacred, unchangeable quality, which obviates the need for further justification – the rule is valid because it *is* a rule. Similarly, Kohlberg's account of the levels of moral reasoning shows that, at the early stages of moral development, children judge an action to be right or wrong in terms of consequent punishment or reward, often conferred by a disapproving or approving authority. But if this is correct, how can moral education ever get going at all? If children can learn their earliest rules and principles only in this way, as the arbitrary edicts of an authority, this seems to be directly opposed to the very idea of moral education. It is as if science teachers found that, for psychological reasons, they had to start teaching science by using methods which contradict the procedures of scientific reasoning (for example, by getting children to ignore the results of experiments, or to invent whatever 'observations' they like).

This puzzle has been called the 'paradox of moral education', and more will be said about it later in section 5.4. In the present context, however, we need to note first that, if Piaget and Kohlberg are right, appeals to authority may be unavoidable when dealing with young children; secondly, that it would not necessarily be surprising or paradoxical to discover that children have to pass through certain 'non-moral' stages of thinking before they can get to grips with morality proper; and thirdly, that if we wish children to come to exercise their own moral judgement at *some* stage (as distinct from blindly obeying an authority), it would seem that to offer simple, reasoned justifications for rules even to young children can at worst do no harm, and may at best encourage the gradual development of more rational moral thinking.

Reflecting upon children's moral learning, then, further clarifies the notion of a 'moral authority', and suggests that authoritative guidance of some kind, far from being incompatible with learning to be moral, is a necessary part of it. 'Teaching' itself implies the exercise of various forms of authority (see Peters 1966, ch. IX), so 'teaching children to be good' can hardly be a totally non-authoritative business, even though morality can never be defined in terms of mere obedience to authority.

There remains a further way, however, in which the content of morality and moral education might be thought definable by means of an appeal to authority, and this must be briefly considered before we proceed to the next section. The authority in this case is not represented by some person, institution, or text, but by the *internal* 'voice of conscience', which many would claim is our supreme (or only) guide to what is morally right or wrong. Conscience is often pictured as a kind of judge or umpire, or as Ryle describes it, a private monitor pronouncing verdicts upon our behaviour (1971, p. 185). Our conscience judges both what we have done in the past and what we intend to do in the future. We often think of it as literally *telling* us what to do, and see ourselves as obeying or disobeying it. The image, then, is of an internalized authority figure, eloquently described by Bishop Butler as follows: 'You cannot form a notion of this faculty, conscience, without taking in judgement, direction, superintendency. This is a constituent part of the idea ... Had it strength, as it has right; had it power as it has manifest authority; it would absolutely govern the world' (1897, p. 55).

But does conscience really represent an authority which can define morality for us? The main difficulty here is that 'conscience' is a highly ambiguous term, which is used to refer to two very different things. On the one hand, there is the 'irrational' sense of conscience, about which Freud in particular had much to say (see Flugel 1945, ch. II–VI). This refers to certain supposed mechanisms by which the young child comes to 'identify' with various commands, prohibitions and values of the parent, and 'internalizes' them with the result that he later (perhaps even as an adult) experiences guilt reactions and feelings of anxiety when he contravenes these rules that he has unconsciously assimilated. On the other hand, however, there is a 'rational' sense of conscience which we use to denote the making of deliberate, conscious, moral judgements about our past, present and future actions. This is well described by Kolnai as 'conscience in the established and dignified sense of moral self-criticism, judgement and belief – which . . . expresses the agent's endeavour to ponder and argue his decisions in universally valid terms and to make his conduct *justifiable* in the open court of objective morality' (1957–8, p. 179, italics in original).

This distinction in effect destroys the image of conscience as a distinctive source of moral authority, for in neither sense can conscience properly be said to be performing this role. As far as 'irrational' conscience is concerned, this has no more to do with *morality* as such than does the colour of our hair, or the size of our feet, or any other personal characteristic with which we happen to have grown up. Feeling unreasonable guilt as an adult in certain situations, as a possible result of our weaning and toilet-training as a baby, tells us nothing about the *moral* features of those situations, just as shuddering at the sight of a snake tells us nothing about how we ought morally to treat snakes. 'Rational' conscience on the other hand, though closely connected with moral reasoning, as Kolnai emphasizes, is hardly to be conceived of as an *authority* requiring *obedience*. The analogy with judges passing verdicts and monitors checking up on our behaviour is misleading here, for there is no 'external' set of standards being applied. 'Rational' conscience refers to *our own* judgements and decisions, made in the light of rules and principles which *we* have freely accepted as morally valid, and have committed *ourselves* to; this makes the idea of conscience as an 'authority', which 'tells' us what to do, both redundant and confusing.

It will accordingly be equally unhelpful to interpret moral education as a process of 'giving a conscience' to children to serve as a moral authority for them. In fact, moral education may actually have to fight *against* children's conscience in the 'irrational' sense, if it is preventing them, because of their early upbringing, from making sensible, realistic appraisals of situations to which they are reacting in rigid, conditioned, unreasonable and guilt-ridden ways. As for 'rational' conscience, helping children to develop this is no doubt an important part of teaching them to become moral agents, but it is less confusing to see the process as one of learning to make *one's own* principled decisions than as one of obeying an authority.

The image of conscience as a prescribing authority, therefore, does not help much in clarifying our view of morality or moral education, but it does at least draw attention to one important element, already noted in our examination of emotivism – the 'feeling' component. The notion of conscience emphasizes that moral agents necessarily *care* about moral issues, *feel committed* to moral principles, *regret* moral mistakes and are *ashamed* of moral failings. Any analysis of morality and moral education will have to take account of these 'affective', 'motivational' aspects, and we shall return to these in the final chapter.

5.2 *Appeals to nature*

Although the content of morality cannot be defined by appealing to the fact that certain authorities prescribe certain rules, might there not be other kinds of fact which can do this job for us? If, for instance, moral questions arise only within the context of man's interaction with his social and physical environment, should we not look to the facts about the nature of man and the world he inhabits for clues to the nature of morality?

This proposal lies at the heart of the ethical theory known as naturalism. There are many versions of this theory, because there are many possible sets of 'natural facts' about man and his environment which can be picked out as being of particular moral significance. Many of these versions are the product of unexamined, 'common-sense' assumptions about morality, rather than of philosophical analysis, but philosophers such as G. E. Moore and R. M. Hare have been active in criticizing these, and have developed their own theories often in reaction to naturalism.

The clearest example of naturalism to start with is the view that certain actions, dispositions, or states of affairs can be classified as 'natural' and 'unnatural', and consequently as 'moral' and 'immoral'. Under the 'natural' heading might come such things as the maintenance of family bonds, or the creation of a home as opposed to the pursuit of a career (in the case of women), or an assertive as opposed to a submissive attitude (in the case of men), or the free expression of one's emotions; while 'unnatural' might typically be applied to incest, or celibacy, or homosexuality, or contraception, or genetic engineering, or little girls who like playing football. Naturalistic beliefs of this kind identify the moral domain descriptively in terms of man's 'nature' or his relationship to the 'natural' world, and produce evaluative judgements on this basis about what is 'moral' and 'immoral'.

Although naturalism need not be interpreted so literally, this simple equation of the 'moral' with the 'natural' provides a good starting-point for us, as it highlights features which are also to be found in more sophisticated versions of the theory. To begin with, there is the obvious difficulty of defining 'nature' (with a small or large 'n'), and of establishing what exactly is in harmony and disharmony with it. How do we discover what principles 'Nature' prescribes? Do these somehow exist in isolation from our *social* conventions and institutions? The problem becomes more apparent if we develop one of the examples given above. Suppose we believe that an important moral issue concerns the lifestyle of women, and that 'Nature' can in some way supply the necessary rules and principles about what that lifestyle should be. But how are we ever to arrive at some 'pure' rule of Nature (for example, that woman's proper place is in the home, raising a family), which is applicable to *all* women because they *are* women, when we consider the vast social, historical and cultural variations in the way in which the role of women is seen? We cannot point for evidence to, say, a 'natural' maternal or domestic inclination in women, first because not all women appear to have such inclinations, and secondly because, even if they did, we could not be sure whether the inclinations had resulted from some 'natural' predisposition, or from *social* expectations and *cultural* conditioning. The enormous diversity of social patterns of behaviour revealed by anthropologists underlines the difficulty, and perhaps the impossibility, of generalizing about the 'nature' of men and women.

Yet even if such generalizations could be safely made, naturalism would face a still more fundamental objection, for why should what is 'natural' be thought to have any necessary connection with what is 'moral', in either the evaluative or the descriptive sense? In the first place, to call something 'natural' is not necessarily to *evaluate* it as being morally praiseworthy. Some of the most likely examples of 'natural' human characteristics would include such dispositions as jealousy, aggression, insecurity, possessiveness and self-centredness, but what is morally desirable about these? Freud would have maintained that it was 'natural' for baby boys to want to kill their fathers and sleep with their mothers, but even if he was right we are not forced to conclude that patricide and incest are a good thing, morally speaking. And in the second place, the same example shows that the area of morality likewise cannot be *descriptively* demarcated in terms of 'natural' laws and principles, for the principle which Freud claimed to have discovered about babies' inclinations is surely a *psychological* rather than a *moral* one. Beliefs about the existence of 'natural' human characteristics can certainly *create* moral problems (such as how should we *treat* patricidally inclined infants, aggressive teenagers, possessive girlfriends, or jealous husbands), but these become moral questions not because of the so-called 'naturalness' of the behaviour in question, but because the issues raised are concerned with personal relationships and principles of interpersonal conduct.

This literal version of naturalism fails, therefore, because it cannot convincingly demonstrate first what counts as 'natural', and secondly why anything defined as 'natural' should be equated with what is moral or morally good. The second type of objection can also be levelled against other versions of naturalism which depend less directly upon the obscure concept of 'natural'.

Naturalism is in fact usually taken by philosophers to refer to any ethical theory which holds that morality is to be defined in terms of some state of affairs which can be *factually described*. Clearly, any alleged facts about 'human nature' will fall under this heading; but so also will a wide range of other facts about man and society, concerning such matters as human survival, social cohesion, political policies, cultural achievements, physical and mental health, national prestige, and so on. We cannot examine all of these alternatives (and there are many more), and need not do so, in order to note that in each case the content of morality will be spelt out in a set of principles applying to one limited aspect only of human and social life. So, for example, the fact that some people seem to live longer, or have fewer mental breakdowns, or produce greater works of art, because they have adopted a particular style of life, might be appealed to in support of a conception of morality centred upon the promotion of that style of life. Or the fact that some tribes maintain their numbers by means of certain fertility rituals, or that some countries maintain full employment by means of certain economic policies, might be used to attribute moral significance to those social and political procedures. The fact that Britannia ruled the waves (when she really did) was often taken to indicate the *moral* character of the British, and their virtual monopoly of the moral as well as the maritime area.

The standard philosophical objection to this kind of argument is that it embodies a fallacy – the 'naturalistic fallacy'. This term was first used by Moore (1903), but is now often applied to a famous section of David Hume's *Treatise of Human Nature*. A whole body of philosophical literature has now developed devoted to examining the naturalistic fallacy in general and Moore's and Hume's arguments in particular (see Hudson 1969). This is not the place to become submerged in problems of interpretation, however, as the main direction of the anti-naturalism attack is both clear and fairly widely accepted by modern philosophers, however obscurely it may have been expressed originally.

The attack rests upon a distinction which can supposedly be drawn between the factual description of a state of affairs and the moral evaluation of that state of affairs, or between statements about what *is* the case and statements about what *ought* to be done. The naturalistic fallacy is committed, it is claimed, when this distinction is blurred by naturalism's assumption that moral conclusions can be directly derived from factual statements. So, for example, the argument would go, the *fact* that women are able to bear children for about thirty years of their life cannot be taken by itself to show that women *ought* to spend these years in constant child-rearing; nor can the *fact* that sadists like inflicting pain on others establish that they *ought* to be allowed to hurt anyone they choose. In all such cases, before a moral 'ought-type' conclusion can be drawn, a *further* moral judgement or assumption has to be made (for example, that all women *ought* to make use of all their physical potentialities all the time, or that sadists *ought* to have their desires satisfied); and this seems to prove what Hume is thought (by some of his readers at least) to have maintained – namely, that it is logically impossible to get an 'ought' directly from an 'is', and that there must always remain a logical gap between statements of fact and judgements of value. There are, then, powerful arguments against the naturalistic view that the moral domain can be defined purely by reference to facts about man and the world, and that the content of morality can be discovered simply by studying what *is* the case.

We can now appreciate the range and importance of naturalistic theories, for even appeals to authority and to conscience, which we examined in section 5.1, could be included within this category, in so far as they try to derive the content of morality from the *fact* that a particular authority or 'inner voice' prescribes a certain set of rules. Some moral philosophers, however, have attempted to produce more refined versions of naturalistic theories, which are possibly more difficult to dismiss as victims of the naturalistic fallacy, and these will be scrutinized in the next section (5.3). Let us first, though, turn to see how naturalism, as it has so far been portrayed, is linked to certain conceptions of moral education.

The clearest examples of approaches to moral education with underlying naturalistic assumptions stem from the more literal versions of the theory, which appeal directly to the facts of 'Nature' or 'children's nature'. Not only moral education but educational theory generally has often shown evidence of such naturalistic influences, usually in the form of a 'child-centred' ideology. Rousseau's educational prescriptions, for instance, were founded upon a belief in the innate goodness of human nature: 'Let us lay it down as an incontestable principle that the first impulses of nature are always right' (1961, p. 56). Or coming nearer to home, we find the prestigious and (one would have expected) more sober-minded government report of the Plowden Committee on Primary Education beginning its survey with the words: 'At the heart of the educational process lies the child. No advances in policy, no acquisitions of new equipment have their desired effect unless they are in harmony with *the nature of the child*, unless they are fundamentally acceptable to him' (1967, para. 9, my italics).

As for the specific teaching of morality, naturalistic theories tend to produce a vision of moral education as a process of inner growth rather than external imposition. Thus, Rousseau emphasized the need for 'negative education' in the earlier years of childhood, when no verbal moral instruction was to be given and no punishment inflicted, so avoiding the inculcation of habits and prejudices; instead, the child was to be left to discover the 'natural consequence' of his actions for himself (1961, bk 2). Similarly, we saw in the previous chapter how Neill emphasized the value of the child's free choice, because 'only under freedom can he grow in *his natural way – the good way*' (1968, p. 108, my italics). Neill believed that it is 'moral instruction that makes the child bad' (p. 221), and that no child should be forced to 'adopt values that he is not *naturally* ready to adopt' (p. 224, my italics). His identification of goodness with 'Nature' is well summed up when he is describing the child's 'natural life force': 'The Church would call the voice of Nature the voice of the devil, and the voice of moral instruction the voice of God. I am convinced that the names should be reversed' (p. 221).

But why should they be reversed? Why should we assume that the 'voice of Nature' or the child's 'natural life force' (whatever these might be) has any *moral* signficance? It is easy to detect the naturalistic fallacy here in the way that Neill appears to deduce moral judgements from factual statements. The so-called 'facts of nature' are in themselves morally neutral, however, in that they can have either a positive or a negative value placed upon them – a point neatly illustrated by Mr Brocklehurst in the novel *Jane Eyre*, when he objects to a pupil in his school having curls in her hair and, on being told that the girl's hair curls *naturally*, replies, 'Naturally! Yes, but we are not to conform to nature: I wish these girls to be the children of Grace.' Mr Brocklehurst, unlike Neill, grasps the logical point that a value judgement has always to be made *about* the facts, 'natural' or otherwise, because the facts themselves cannot determine the content of morality or moral education.

It is for this reason also that another naturalistic approach to moral education must be deemed inadequate. 'Moral education' seldom appears as such on the school timetable, and with the ever-growing pressure of other competing subjects there is often a strong temptation for headteachers to assume that moral questions are being satisfactorily 'covered' under other headings, such as social studies, environmental studies, political education, health education, or sex education – or even some combination of all these, parading under the title of 'personal and social education.' Yet in so far as these other subjects remain descriptive and factual, they cannot of themselves provide any distinctively *moral* content. Factual information about how pollution occurs, how political institutions work, how babies are conceived, and so on, cannot in itself yield moral rules or principles without running foul of the naturalistic fallacy. Knowing the facts is, of course, important when making moral judgements, but learning how to make these judgements is by no means the same thing as learning the facts. Merely teaching children facts, therefore, will teach them nothing about morality as such. Moral questions can, needless to say, be raised and discussed in connection with various political, environmental, social, or biological facts, but it is precisely at this point that moral education must make its own distinctive contribution, and not be subsumed under other purely empirical subjects. This was one of the reasons why it was suggested in Chapter 2 that the growing emphasis upon 'personal and social education' with no explicit acknowledgement of its unavoidably *moral* foundations could be a confusing and dangerous development. Teachers as well as philosophers, then, need to be aware of the distinction between 'is' and 'ought', and to appreciate the limitations of naturalism, when considering what the content of moral education should be.

5.3 *Appeals to human welfare*

While few moral philosophers would today want to defend the kinds of naturalistic theory which have so far been described, there has in recent years been much philosophical debate about whether one particular set of alleged 'facts' can succeed in defining the content of morality – 'facts' about *human welfare*. Again the arguments have been lengthy and complex, and all that can be given here is an outline of the main points at issue.

Attempts to establish some distinctively moral rules and principles by appealing to the notion of human welfare have taken various forms. Some philosophers have tried to invoke a 'principle of utility', claiming that an action becomes moral when it is *useful* in promoting human benefit; so morality's rules and principles must be those which are concerned with increasing the sum of human happiness and pleasure, and reducing the sum of human misery and pain. Others have placed the emphasis upon rather more specific principles, such as the satisfaction of human *needs*, or the fulfilment of human *wants* and *desires*, or the consideration of human *interests*.

These accounts usually share two common features. First, they claim that the term 'moral', as used in everyday language, actually does refer in all cases to matters of human welfare. G. J. Warnock, for example, argues: 'Must it not surely be supposed, by anyone who claims to be propounding a moral principle, that observance of the principle he propounds would do some sort of *good*, and that breaches of it would do some sort of *harm*?' (1967, p. 55, italics in original). Secondly, they maintain that there exist indisputable *facts* about human welfare, which can be objectively agreed upon; to quote Warnock again: 'At least some questions as to what is good or bad for people, what is harmful or beneficial, are not in any serious sense matters of opinion. That it is a bad thing to be tortured or starved, humiliated or hurt, is not an opinion: it is a fact' (ibid., p. 60). Morality, then, is by definition concerned with questions of human good and harm, and these questions can be answered *factually*. Foot, whose work in this area has attracted a lot of attention, sums up the argument neatly: 'It is surely clear that moral virtues must be connected with human good and harm, and that it is quite impossible to call anything you like good or harm' (1967, p. 92).

This kind of description of morality sounds highly convincing, probably because it is in accord with many of our 'common-sense' beliefs and assumptions about the matter. In practice, most of us no doubt do make many of our moral decisions on the basis of some such 'utilitarian' principle, involving calculations of what we think will produce the most benefit (or the least harm) for everyone concerned; and surely there are undeniable facts about what actually does benefit and harm people, about what causes pleasure and pain. So is it not merely perverse to try and deny that there are such things as 'moral facts' about human welfare, which can supply the distinctive content of morality?

What we take to be 'common sense', however, is not always as self-evidently correct as it appears to be, and if we examine the above argument more closely, we find that both of its main planks are suspect.

First, can morality be adequately defined in terms of human welfare? Certainly it would be very odd to suggest that morality had *nothing* to do with human good and harm, but is that *all* that it can be to do with? Again we have the problem of deciding whether this proposed feature is a necessary characteristic of every aspect of morality, and again we must conclude that it is not. Why, for example, is it only *human* welfare that is specified? What about the welfare of *non*-humans, such as animals, plant-life, or bug-eyed monsters from outer space (if and when we ever meet any)? Are there not moral questions about how we ought to treat animals, what we ought and ought not to do to our natural environment, and how we ought to behave towards any extra-terrestrial beings who might contact us? None of these issues is concerned with *human* welfare as such – in fact they acquire their moral quality precisely when the over-riding importance of human welfare is called into question (when, for example, we *disregard* the 'benefits' which factory-farming has brought to mankind, and ask, 'But is it really *right* to treat animals like that, however much we humans may gain from it?').

Alternatively, if the content of morality is to be restricted to considerations about the welfare of other human beings, what is my position as a moral agent if I am marooned alone on a desert island, with no hope of rescue or contact with other people, or if I find myself the sole survivor of a global nuclear war or natural catastrophe? Am I automatically removed from the sphere of morality because there are no other human beings whose welfare I can consider? Would I not still have moral decisions to make about how I should spend my time, think my thoughts, and interact with the natural world?

Finally, to define morality in this way ignores the fact that what appear to be some clear examples of moral rules and principles have little direct connection with human welfare, and may easily lead to an overall *decrease* in human happiness on many occasions. Truth-telling and promise-keeping, for instance, are usually held to be moral matters, *regardless* of whether anyone benefits or gains pleasure from them. Similarly, what many have held to be the supreme moral principle, that of justice, is hardly a guaranteed recipe for happiness. In Terence Rattigan's play *The Winslow Boy*, for example, a father fights a long legal battle to clear the name of his son, who has been accused of petty theft; his decision that justice must be done *at all costs* is surely a moral one, although it is not taken with the intention of increasing anyone's happiness, and in fact creates much tension and anxiety for all concerned. Or again, some see it as morally necessary to hunt down senile Nazi war criminals in the name of justice, though it is not obvious what human benefit would result from their capture.

The area of morality, then, seems to be wider than that encompassed merely by principles concerning the facts of human welfare. Moreover, the second stage of the argument can also be challenged by querying whether there really are any *facts* as such of this kind. Appeals to human welfare as the corner-stone of morality try in effect to bridge the gap between 'is' and 'ought', and so avoid the naturalistic fallacy, but many philosophers would maintain that these attempts fail because the so-called 'factual' descriptions of human welfare do not really rely upon facts at all, but upon hidden value judgements.

This objection becomes clearer when we ask what the 'facts' of human welfare really are. Phillips and Mounce argue in an important article: 'There is no common agreement on what constitutes human good and harm ... [for] human good is not independent of the moral beliefs people hold, but is determined by them' (1969, p. 234). Using the example of a Roman Catholic housewife in disagreement with a scientific rationalist over the question of birth control and size of family, they conclude that no appeal to the 'facts' can resolve the dispute: 'There is no settling of the issue in terms of some supposed common evidence called human good and harm, since what they differ over is precisely the question of what constitutes human good and harm' (ibid., p. 239).

The naturalistic fallacy, then, cannot be by-passed so easily. A descriptive statement (for example, he has lost an eye) always needs the addition of a *non*-factual value judgement (it is bad to lose an eye) in order to produce the so-called 'moral fact' (he has been harmed by losing an eye), and it is always possible to question the value judgement and thereby disprove the 'moral fact' (by following the biblical advice in Matthew's gospel to pluck out your eye if it offends you: 'It is better to enter into life with one eye, rather than having two eyes to be cast into hell fire'). One can always ask, of *any* human state, 'What's good (or bad) about that?' and while this may seem a heartless question in some circumstances, it is not a meaningless one; and the fact that it is not meaningless shows that there must always exist a distinction between describing a state of affairs and morally evaluating it. Facts alone cannot produce moral principles.

Nor is the objection overcome by trying to make a 'moral fact' out of human *happiness* or *satisfaction*, for again we can always ask 'What's good about that?' Normally, of course, we consider it a good thing for people to be happy and have their desires satisfied, but this hardly applies to megalomaniacs and rapists, so how can it be a 'moral fact'? What is more, even apparently factual statements about a person's happiness often carry with them evaluative overtones. As Hare remarks, we object to calling a person happy if we *disapprove* of his decisions and his desires, even if the latter have been satisfied: 'This explains why, for example, few of us would say that an opium addict was happy (*really* happy) if he always got enough opium' (1963, p. 128, italics in original).

Appealing to the so-called 'facts' about human welfare, then, does not succeed in defining the content of morality, first because moral questions are not limited just to that area, and secondly because there do not seem to be any pure, non-evaluative 'facts' of this kind to appeal to.

In view of these objections to what initially sounds a convincing description of morality, it is important to examine particularly closely any account of moral education that seems to be based on this kind of foundation. We do not have to look far for an example, as the Schools Council Project in Moral Education, already mentioned in Chapters 2 and 4, clearly comes into this category, illustrating how programmes of moral education rest upon particular, theoretical assumptions about the nature of morality, and how any flaws in those assumptions can be transferred to the programme's practical recommendations.

The overall aim of the project, as we have seen, is to encourage boys and girls to 'live well' and to adopt a 'considerate style of life' (McPhail, Ungoed-Thomas and Chapman 1972, p. 3). No one, of course, would want to deny that consideration for others should be emphasized in any moral education programme. A person who was consistently inconsiderate and insensitive to the feelings of others could hardly qualify as being morally educated. Yet the two main objections we have noted to ethical theories appealing to the 'facts' of human welfare apply with equal force to McPhail's account of moral education.

In the first place, considerateness cannot be set up as the *sole* principle of morality, or as the *sole* aim of moral education. There are other possible areas of morality, as we have seen, which might invoke principles of justice, honour, personal integrity, perseverance, self-denial, or self-development, and even if a teacher does not himself value these as highly as considerateness, that is no justification for presenting a programme of moral education which concentrates upon the one preferred principle to the exclusion of all the others. The teacher of any subject has the duty of presenting a reasonably broad spectrum of that subject to his pupils; to teach that history is all about the British Empire, or that biology is all about the theory of evolution, or that religion is all about the Church of England, comes close to indoctrination.

In the second place, McPhail appears to derive his principle of considerateness from various sets of 'facts', so disguising the value judgements which he cannot avoid making, and claiming an objective, empirical basis for his programme which it does not in fact possess. The principle, for example, is said to have been discovered from the results of a pilot study, which surveyed the opinions of some teenagers on the question of what they considered to be examples of 'good' and 'bad' behaviour by adults and adolescents. This revealed that '"good" treatment was that which showed consideration for another's needs, interests and feelings, "bad" treatment was that which did not' (ibid., p. 46). However, the mere fact that several hundred English schoolchildren in the second half of the twentieth century happen to use 'good' and 'bad' in these ways cannot establish that morality is therefore necessarily all about considerateness. If the survey had shown that the majority of teenagers questioned thought that 'good' behaviour consisted in throwing your weight about and getting what you want at any cost, would McPhail have constructed his moral education programme upon *those* principles? Presumably not – so the 'facts' about how children use 'good' and 'bad' cannot automatically yield the content of moral education.

A further set of 'facts' which McPhail uses to arrive at his principle of considerateness reveals an equally dubious argument: 'An individual's considerate style of life', he maintains, 'is productive of happiness and health for that individual because it earns acceptance and supporting feedback, because it reduces stress' (ibid., p. 8). So the 'facts' which are here being used to prove the moral importance of considerateness refer to *one's own* welfare and happiness: 'When boys and girls adopt a considerate style of life, not only do others benefit but they themselves gain in a number of important ways' (p. 3). But to rely in this way upon the alleged (and highly disputable) 'fact' that one stands to profit from being considerate to others surely robs McPhail's account of its *moral* dimensions; for to say, 'I'm acting like this because of what I'm going to get out of it', is not to give a *moral* reason for whatever one is doing. Indeed, many would argue that one distinguishing feature of a moral action is precisely that it is *not* performed with the intention of gaining some reward or avoiding some punishment. Yet, according to McPhail, morality is a kind of fruit-machine which never fails to pay out, and it is the job of moral education to get children to keep pulling the handle in order to collect their guaranteed winnings. Again we must ask whether, if the 'facts' happened to be different and showed that considerateness did *not* pay for most people, but that insensitivity and exploitation reaped handsome rewards, McPhail would place *those* principles at the centre of his moral education programme.

This attempt, then, to base moral education upon the 'facts' of human welfare produces an edifice which is logically very shaky indeed. That is not to deny that the encouragement of a considerate attitude may be an essential element in moral education, nor that the project may have devised some stimulating teaching materials – but without a clear appraisal of the ethical theory on which it is founded and the pitfalls therein, any such programme can only be whistling in the dark.

5.4 *Appeals to reason*

If neither the pronouncements of authorities nor the 'facts' about nature and human welfare can supply the content of moral rules and principles, what other source can we look to? Many philosophers have held that morality is essentially a *rational* matter, and that reasoned justification forms its central core. Some have gone further still, by trying to deduce a set of specific principles which they claim form part of the meaning of morality, as a result of its rational character.

An influential, recent argument of this kind has been that put forward by Peters, whose theory is of special interest for our purposes, as he has discussed at length its implications for moral education. Peters's starting-point is what he calls the activity of 'practical discourse' or 'practical reason': 'The situation postulated is one in which any individual, possessed of a public language, asks the question "What ought I to do?" There are alternatives open to him and he is asking for reasons for adopting one alternative rather than another' (1966, p. 121). If a person is 'seriously discussing with others or with himself what he ought to do' (p. 115), Peters maintains that he is thereby accepting the importance of seeking reasons for action, and is also acknowledging implicitly the validity of certain moral principles.

For example, the principle of fairness or justice can be established in this way, because by searching for reasons why one should treat somebody in one way rather than another (for example, whether a teacher should give the same reward or punishment to an intelligent girl as to a backward boy for a particular piece of good or bad behaviour), one is tacitly granting that different forms of treatment are justified only if different situational factors exist; in other words, fairness *means* treating people in the same way unless there are relevant differences between them, and looking for these relevant differences is an integral part of considering seriously what one ought to do. Using a similar form of argument, Peters also deduces the principles of truth-telling, freedom, consideration of others' interests and respect for persons. Truth-telling becomes a necessary moral principle, because for a person seriously to ask 'What ought I to do?'

presupposes that he is concerned to pursue and discover the truth; freedom, because anyone seriously asking the question must expect non-interference when doing what he decides there are good reasons for doing; consideration of others' interests, because asking the question also implies that people's claims and concerns about what is worthwhile will be taken into account; and respect for persons, because in asking the question one is committing oneself to listening to what other people have to say about the matter and respecting their point of view.

These are, needless to say, principles of a very general nature, which do not provide straightforward, indisputable answers to questions about what one ought to do in any particular situation. To implement the principle of fairness, for example, one will have to decide what counts as a 'relevant difference' between two people, which might justify treating them differently; the principle alone will not tell a teacher, for instance, how to treat children of different abilities, backgrounds, ages and sex within the same class or group. It is also quite possible that some of the principles may conflict on occasions; telling the truth may not always be thought compatible with considering others' interests, as we saw earlier. These practical problems, however, do not pose any real threat to Peters's position, for he is not claiming to provide a moral instruction manual with ready-made answers for all contingencies, but rather a general framework of guiding principles which all moral deliberation must take into account.

The main objection that Peters's theory does have to face concerns the notion of 'seriously asking the question what I ought to do', from which all the principles are derived. When can I actually be said to be asking the question 'seriously'? Presumably only when I do in fact accept the validity of the various principles – but this seems to be a circular argument, which merely *defines* 'seriously' in terms of commitment to those principles, thereby denying that anyone not so committed can count as 'serious'. Yet might I not claim to be asking the question seriously (in the normal sense of the word) *without* any such moral overtones or implications? Perhaps I am seriously deliberating what I ought to do about providing for my old age, or creating an artistic masterpiece, or getting the new batsman out before he settles down; in none of these cases need my seriousness imply any commitment to Peters's principles of fairness, respect for persons, and so on. Can I not, then, ask the question seriously, yet remain outside the boundaries of morality and the jurisdiction of Peters's principles?

Furthermore, if a person refuses or does not bother to ask the question 'seriously' in the first place, the rules of morality which Peters deduces cannot apply to him, because he is not, as it were, playing the moral game. He might simply pursue his own interests, satisfy his own desires, and not concern himself with what he ought (morally) to do, thereby avoiding any acknowledgement of Peters's principles – though he could still, of course, seriously consider what he ought to do about improving his sun-tan or his golf-swing.

The main difficulty about Peters's argument, then, is that one has to be a moral agent *already*, before its force can be felt. Once I am in the (moral) position of 'seriously' asking questions about what I (morally) ought to do, then I may well be implicitly accepting that there are necessary, moral principles of the kind which Peters describes, but I have to be playing the moral game before I can see the point of its rules. This clearly imposes some limitations on the scope of the theory, but the fact remains that the vast majority of people do qualify as moral agents, in the sense that they sometimes ask moral questions and make moral decisions, though they are often unclear as to what sort of reasons count as morally relevant in deciding what they ought to do. In this situation Peters's account is particularly helpful, as it draws the attention of the moral agent to the hidden implications of asking moral questions, by spelling out a specific set of moral principles to which he must already be committed, perhaps without realizing it.

We are still left, however, with the problem which faces all content-based descriptions of morality: is there any one principle or set of principles which must be included as a necessary part of all forms of morality? None of Peters's principles would have much application to the desert island castaway, or the global holocaust survivor, or the outer space explorer, or the animal-lover, whom we discussed in the previous section, yet these people surely still have moral decisions to make. These are, however, admittedly extreme examples, and while we must bear them in mind as an indication of morality's broad dimensions, it is clear that most moral questions are concerned with interpersonal relationships of some kind, and it is here that Peters's *rational, social* conception of morality and of moral discourse is most relevant.

Peters has also had much to say about the business of moral education, for his account of morality suggests some particular problems likely to be encountered in teaching children to be good. We have already seen that his theory presupposes a moral agent asking 'serious' moral questions and following the rules of the moral game, but how do children learn to play this game? Morality, according to Peters, is based upon a set of rationally deduced and justified principles, so moral education must be a matter of getting children to adopt these principles, though not in a rigid or unreasoning way: 'My concern', says Peters, 'is for the development of an *autonomous* type of character who follows rules in a *rational discriminating* manner...He must not only come to know what is in general right or wrong; he must also go beyond the level of what Plato called ὀρθη δόξα [*orthe doxa*, correct opinion], so that he sees *why* such rules are right and wrong and can *revise* rules and make new ones in the light of new knowledge and new circumstances' (1974, pp. 253–4, my italics).

How can children be encouraged to develop towards this level? This is where the 'paradox of moral education', already mentioned in section 5.1, again rears its head, for the difficulty here is that young children are far from being rational, autonomous characters, able to appreciate that reasons can justify rules and that rules can be impartially evaluated and revised: 'The brute facts of child development reveal that at the most formative years of a child's development he is incapable of this form of life and impervious to the proper manner of passing it on' (ibid., p. 271). It is for this reason that Peters believes that *habit formation* must play an essential part in the moral development of young children: 'They can and must enter the palace of Reason through the courtyard of Habit and Tradition' (ibid., p. 272). So children must be taught a set of 'basic rules', which they come to adopt as habits in as rational a manner as is possible for them at that time, until they are able to think more critically about how such rules might be justified.

But how are we to decide what these 'basic rules' are to be? Again we are faced with the problem of defining a content for morality, but Peters sees no great difficulty here, claiming that there is considerable agreement 'between reflective people' about what the 'basic rules' are: those concerning contracts, property, the care of the young and the avoidance of pain and injury (ibid., pp. 285, 365). These rules, in Peters's view, are necessary for any tolerable form of social life, and are closely connected with the more general moral principles already mentioned.

There is probably more room for disagreement here than Peters allows over which 'basic rules' children should be taught. His list is a short one, which could hardly constitute an adequate moral code for young children, yet even this limited set of rules may not be accepted by all 'reflective people' as being unquestionably moral. Bring together a group of parents which includes some Marxists, some squatters, some gipsies, some landed gentry, some fundamentalist Christians and some child-centred atheists, all of whom would of course claim to be 'reflective people', and you are not likely to find much agreement over particular rules about property, contracts and the care of the young, even if they all accept the general principles which Peters enumerates. So how are we to decide upon a commonly agreed set of moral rules to which children should become habituated in the early stages of their moral development?

Despite these difficulties, which tend to confront any content-based theory of morality and moral education, Peters's work in this area (which is far more wide-ranging and sophisticated than this brief summary suggests) is extremely useful to our investigation. In particular, the way in which he tries to reconcile his account of morality with the facts of child development, and so produce a realistic picture of how moral education might proceed, illustrates well how philosophical questions have to be asked about the nature of morality itself before we can decide whether or not we can teach children to be good.

We have now looked at a representative sample of content-based accounts of morality and moral education, as we did with the formal accounts, though there has been no attempt to conduct a comprehensive survey of all possible ethical theories, as this would be for our present purposes both tedious and unnecessary.

As in the previous chapter, no conclusive answers about the nature and meaning of morality have emerged, but a further set of features has come to light which, though not sufficient in itself to provide a full description of the moral area, helps us to understand more of its logical geography. The range of contexts, for example, in which moral issues can arise is so broad that it seems doubtful whether any one rule or principle, or set of rules and principles, can be shown to be applicable to all of them. Most widely applicable are probably those dealing with the promotion of human welfare and consideration for others, but even here we have seen that there are great problems of interpretation in particular situations, and agreement cannot be reached by a mere appeal to the 'facts'. Moral rules and principles cannot be empirically established as right or wrong; all that seems possible is some attempt at critical, rational justification, and we have noted how Peters tries to arrive at certain social principles of interpersonal conduct in this way.

This chapter has also been salutary in demonstrating how a number of influential and widely held views about moral education rest upon suspect theoretical foundations. Furthermore, although rules and principles seem to form a necessary part of the content of morality, there are difficult questions to be answered about *which* rules and principles children should be taught, and how they should be taught them. These and other questions about the teaching of morality will, however, be easier to tackle in the final chapter now that we have a clearer idea of the problems surrounding the meaning of morality.

6: So Can We Teach Children To Be Good?

Much more has been achieved in the previous two chapters than a mere survey of what some philosophers have had to say about the meaning of morality. We have also seen how different definitions produce different descriptions of moral education, how the nature of morality can be clarified by considering ways in which it might be taught and learned, and how our attitudes towards moral education presuppose beliefs and assumptions about morality itself, which have often not been examined with sufficient rigour.

The particular danger has emerged of failing to realize that so great a diversity of viewpoints does actually exist, and of thereby taking it for granted that there is no problem about the meaning of morality or of moral education. Several examples have been given of practical approaches to moral education which reveal how easy it is to argue persuasively for a certain method of teaching children about morality without realizing the serious objections that can be raised against the single, definitive account of morality, *assumed* by the proponent of the argument to be unquestionable.

Yet teachers and parents have in the end to come to some decisions about whether they can and should try to teach children to be good, and they will never do this by continuing to sit on the fence indefinitely, fearful of reaching any conclusions because of the complexities of the problem. In this final chapter, therefore, the strategy will be to draw upon a selection of the material which has been discussed in the preceding chapters, in order to offer some tentative answers to those questions which teachers and parents cannot avoid: what should children be taught about morality, and how should they be taught it?

6.1 Form and content

Before we can decide *what* we should try to teach, we must first resolve the form-versus-content issue, as the subject matter of moral education obviously must reflect what is characteristic of morality itself. If we are to increase children's understanding of the moral area, therefore, and encourage them to develop as moral agents, do we teach them some 'distinctive' method of moral reasoning, or some 'distinctive' set of moral rules and principles?

Two general points about form and content can be deduced from the previous two chapters. In the first place, it seems impossible to specify any one particular form or content which decisively marks out all the external boundaries and internal landmarks of the moral territory. Morality just does not appear to be like that. As G. J. Warnock remarks, '"moral" is surely not, on any showing, a very exact word, or a word to be always very confidently applied or withheld' (1967, p. 59). The problem is that some accounts which we have looked at propose features which can be found in the *non-moral* as well as the moral area (for example, prescriptivity and principle application), while others focus upon elements which are not common to *all* aspects of morality (for example, principles concerning human happiness or interpersonal consideration). In the second place, the distinction between form and content, though useful in clarifying our thoughts about how to define morality, is less sharp than at first appears. There is in fact considerable overlap between the two in some of the theories we have studied. Does Hare's principle of universality, or Peters's principle of fairness, for example, really describe the *form* that moral reasoning allegedly must take, or the necessary *content* of that reasoning? Are appeals to authority or to human welfare best seen as a *form* of moral justification, or as substantive definitions of morality's *content*? There is no point in agonizing for long over these problems of classification, once we have realized that the distinction itself cannot be pushed too far.

These two points are of great practical importance when we come to make decisions about the subject matter of moral education. While it might be more convenient and satisfying to be able to define the form and/or content of morality as precisely as we can for subjects like geometry or ornithology, the structure and scope of morality are too elastic to allow such precise analysis. Morality's form and content are multifaceted, and the most we can do is to take note of as many of the facets as possible, and see how they interconnect to illuminate morality's many sides. We can only attempt to identify its most typical features, without pretending that we have thereby succeeded in laying down a conclusive set of necessary and sufficient conditions. These 'typical features' must then somehow be taught to children, if they are to be morally educated, but no stark choice has to be made between teaching *either* the form *or* the content of morality; for if the distinction is so blurred and morality's dimensions are so broad as they appear to be, the subject matter of moral education will be unnecessarily restricted and distorted by being based exclusively on either form or content. Children need to be acquainted with the widest possible range of moral understanding that we can offer.

What, then, are some of the 'typical features' of morality that have emerged, and how can children best be made aware of them? The following thumbnail sketch of how a 'typical' moral decision is made should provide us with some useful pointers. Suppose that a teenager witnesses an example of dangerous driving, in which no one is hurt but he has to decide whether or not to report the incident to the police. If he is to qualify as a moral agent, his decision must be freely taken, intentional and resulting from some degree of independent judgement; he cannot go along to the police just because his father or teacher tells him to do so, nor can he ignore the event just because his friends tell him not to bother about it. He must consider the implications and likely consequences of his decision, trying to visualize how it will affect other people, and what good or harm it may do. He will in this way be seeking reasons to justify his decision, and these reasons must be of a general and disinterested kind; the fact that he happens to be feeling tired, or that he knows the owner of the car, would not be a morally relevant consideration. His reasons will also be expressible in terms of a rule or principle which he is prepared to apply in other similar situations; if he decides that dangerous drivers ought always to be reported, then as a moral agent he is accepting that he, his friends, his parents and anyone else ought to be reported, if they ever drive dangerously. Finally, having made up his mind in this way, he must care enough about the matter to act upon his decision, whatever it is, and do what he judges to be right.

This sketch has quite a lot in common with Wilson's description of the morally educated person, which has been referred to earlier, though Wilson appears to think it not impossible to give an all-embracing account of morality's necessary features (1973). Our own claim is less ambitious, for it must be re-emphasized that our survey implies that a comprehensive picture cannot be painted of *everything* that must feature in *any* moral activity. The above sketch does, however, pick out the main 'typical features' which have so far come to light, thereby offering a reasonable set of objectives for moral education. If we turn now to consider how these objectives might be achieved, it soon becomes obvious that several different forms of teaching will be required. It will be helpful, then, to return to the distinctions drawn in Chapter 1 between teach that..., teaching how...and teaching to..., and to examine in turn the contribution which each of these might make.

6.2 *Teaching that...*

Teaching that certain things are and are not the case is an essential part of moral education, because one cannot make sound moral decisions without a firm basis of factual information. This is not to say, however, that there are 'moral facts' which can directly supply the moral content of what is to be taught, for that possibility was rejected in the previous chapter. The information which the teenager in our last example needs concerns the facts of road safety, the causes of accidents, the injuries which victims can suffer, the penalties which convicted drivers incur, the procedure of reporting an offence to the police, and so on, but these are not 'moral facts' which conclusively establish what he ought to do; rather they are *factors* of which he has to take account in arriving at an informed, rational judgement.

It will not be easy to work out what selection of information is of most use to young people in making moral decisions, as different situations will call for different factual knowledge. All that can be done is to ensure that they have that information which we predict will be of most relevance in those moral situations in which they are most likely to find themselves. Obvious areas where factual information will probably be needed include the following: safety in the home and school and on the roads, for a child's behaviour here can easily affect the lives of others, and of himself; individual and group psychology, for children of all ages need to increase their understanding of why people behave in certain ways in certain circumstances, in order that they may become better at anticipating the feelings and reactions of others, and of themselves; emotional, social, intellectual, physical and sexual development, for it is important that children realize the vast range of human differences which must be taken into account in deciding how to treat other people; and lastly, mental and physical health, for children's interpretations of 'human welfare' must be based on some understanding of what is normally considered to be healthy and beneficial. The list could be extended almost indefinitely, for *all* information is grist to the moral agent's mill, but the above areas at least suggest some starting-points for a planned teaching programme. It is here that the label of 'personal and social education' is perhaps most appropriate, for much of this factual information involves knowledge and understanding about oneself and other people.

Is there also a place in moral education for teaching children that morality is made up of certain *rules* which they must obey? Here we are back with the 'paradox of moral education', and the problem of getting children started on the moral road in such a way as not to retard their later progress as independent travellers. How can we summarize our conclusions abut this form of teaching?

First, young children need to be taught what a rule is, because rules and principles are the medium through which moral language is expressed. Secondly, they will have to be given *examples* of simple rules to follow, before they can begin to formulate any for themselves. Thirdly, there is a number of such 'basic rules' (concerning non-injury, for instance), which only the most perverse of philosophers, or the most permissive of parents, would want to deny should be taught to young children. Fourthly, some form of unsophisticated but reasoned *justification* can and should be given for these rules wherever practicable, even if it takes young children some time to start to appreciate this. And fifthly and finally, children should be taught as early as possible that rules are not proven facts but moral judgements, and as such can be rationally supported, discussed, challenged and perhaps revised; so any moral content that is taught in the form of specific rules must be presented, as it were, *provisionally*, for moral education must aim ultimately at getting children not simply to *obey* certain rules, but to seek the *justification* for them and subject them to rational criticism.

These points indicate that, in practice, teaching that... is often closely intertwined with the second form of teaching – teaching how... Teaching children along the lines just suggested, that there are certain moral rules which should be followed, will soon shade into teaching them *how* to form moral rules and make moral judgements for themselves. Let us turn next, then, to consider the *skills* which have emerged as most important in moral reasoning, and the ways in which they might be taught.

6.3 Teaching how...

The first and most general 'typical feature' of moral reasoning that must be examined from the educational viewpoint concerns the need for some degree of independent judgement and free choice to be exercised in the making of moral decisions. This is such a broad requirement (and also, of course, one which applies not only to the moral area, but to all aspects of rational thinking) that it is unlikely to be *directly* teachable in the way that more specific skills, like tying one's own shoelaces, are – although 'decision-making' is coming to be increasingly thought of as a composite ability which can be taught. Probably, however, the most influential factor in determining the development of this moral component is to be found, not in any particular set of teaching materials, but in the attitude and example of teachers and parents. Making up one's own mind in the light of relevant information, rather than merely doing as one is told, is a procedure which children appear to 'pick up' from adults who practise it themselves and expect others to practise it. Teachers and parents who complain that their children do not or cannot 'think for themselves' tend to be those who, in practice, allow least opportunity for children to work out their own conclusions and make their own decisions. Of course, this can be a time-consuming and irritating business for the adult, much slower than *telling* children what to think and do, but how otherwise are they to get the flavour of what it means to 'think for yourself', and so take the first steps towards becoming autonomous moral agents?

Two particular teaching approaches described in Chapter 2 may be worth considering in this connection. First, value neutrality, as exemplified by the Schools Council Nuffield Humanities Project (2.2), implicitly denies that there are authoritatively 'right' answers to the controversial questions which pupils are encouraged to discuss; the moral agent cannot make his choices and judgements by blindly accepting the pronouncements of an authority figure, nor by merely conforming to the majority view because it *is* the majority view. Value neutrality, then, underlines the importance of independent judgement, and represents a determined attempt to get children to weigh evidence for themselves and reach their own informed conclusions. Secondly, values clarification aims to lead children, by means of dialogue and discussion, to work out what their values are, and why they hold them. Much emphasis here is placed upon free choice; one's values are to be *chosen* from a range of alternatives, as a result of reflecting carefully upon the likely consequences and implications of each alternative, and many 'games' and simulation exercises have been constructed to aid the making of such choices (2.3).

There are, then, some possible teaching strategies which might help children to make their own choices, decisions and judgements; but could any of the more specific, 'typical features' of moral reasoning also be taught as skills? The survey conducted in Chapters 4 and 5 revealed an interrelated cluster of such features, suggesting that moral judgements are typically characterized by their generality, universality, logical consistency, objectivity, detachment and impartiality. We can best summarize what has already been said about these features by pointing out in negative terms what moral reasoning is *not*. The judgements and decisions with which it is concerned cannot be made arbitrarily, without any reference to general rules or principles, nor can they be seen as unrelated to other similar situations, nor can they be viewed as mere expressions of personal whims, tastes, or feelings. Moral reasoning is in these respects an 'impersonal' matter, though paradoxically it is most frequently employed in making decisions about personal relationships, personal interests and personal welfare. Thus, the teenager witnessing the dangerous driving has, in one sense, to make an 'impersonal', moral judgement (that is, one that disregards the *personalities* involved and his own feelings towards them), yet in another sense his decision must take account of how other people's personal well-being will be affected by whatever he does.

The 'impersonal' features of moral reasoning present some interesting teaching problems, particular in connection with the so-called 'egocentric' and 'concrete' thinking of younger children. The ability to reason in general rather than particular terms, and to adopt a detached, impartial viewpoint, appears to develop relatively late, and it is an open question to what extent such abilities can be 'taught'. Kohlberg, for example, argues that direct teaching (though not 'cognitive stimulation', which he somewhat confusingly contrasts with teaching) cannot raise children from a lower to a higher stage of moral thinking (1970, 1976).

Yet certain forms of teaching seem, on the face of it at least, to provide a useful and necessary foundation for some of the skills of moral reasoning. One such approach is exemplified by the familiar response of the reproving teacher or parent – 'What would it be like if *everyone* behaved like that?', or 'How would you feel if some one did that to *you*?' Though the adult asking these questions will often not have worked out the philosophical rationale behind them, this is still an excellent way of drawing a young child's attention to the features of generality and universality, by prompting him to detach himself from his 'self-centred' perspective and try to imagine other viewpoints. Until the child starts to make these thought experiments for himself, by visualizing himself in the position of others, his moral development must be severely limited.

The Schools Council Moral Education Project also makes fruitful suggestions in this connection, despite its suspect theoretical foundations. Both the 'Lifeline' materials, designed for teenagers, and the 'Startline' programme, intended for 8–13-year-olds, lay great emphasis upon the need for children to develop their interpersonal understanding by trying to see other people's points of view and putting themselves into other people's shoes. This 'de-centring' process, whatever effect it may have upon children's 'considerateness', could well lead to the making of more objective and impartial judgements.

Both the above approaches may also help to develop and refine the child's concept of 'fairness' by illustrating the 'impersonality' of moral reasoning. The notion of 'fairness' is itself a crucial one for teachers and parents to focus upon, for it is simultaneously a basic element in even the young child's moral vocabulary and also a moral principle of great philosophical significance. It lies, for example, at the centre of Peters's rationally deduced principles, and neatly encompasses most of the 'impersonal' features of morality that have been mentioned; a 'fair' decision is one which is held to be applicable to other similar situations, is logically coherent and is arrived at in an impartial, non-arbitrary and non-subjective manner. There seems no more promising method, therefore, of giving children the flavour of moral reasoning, and of getting them to practise the skills which it requires, than by taking every opportunity to discuss with them what *counts* as 'fair' and 'unfair', and why. Concrete examples of everyday incidents can be used with young children (for example, is it necessarily fair to punish two children in the same way for the same piece of mis-behaviour?), leading to a consideration of more general applications of the principle at the later, more advanced stages of reasoning (is apartheid a 'fair' system of social organisation?).

Much more detail, of course, needs to be filled into the practical suggestions for teaching that...and teaching how...that have been outlined in this and the previous section, but it seems safe to proceed on the assumption that a sizeable chunk of morality's 'typical' form and content is in fact teachable. Children can be taught a great deal of factual information, which is a prerequisite for making rational moral decisions; they can be taught at a young age certain basic rules, which all or most moral agents would accept and also, at an appropriate level, the reasoning that lies behind them; they can be taught how to start making up their own minds freely and reflectively about moral questions; and they can be taught how to reason about moral matters in a way which respects the 'impersonal' features of morality. These items cannot, needless to say, all be taught directly, straightforwardly, or with the immediate prospect of success. Most of them represent long-term objectives, which may be achieved only after a lengthy period of experience, practice and maturation, as well as teaching. Yet there remains plenty of scope for positive teaching, in familiarizing children with these aspects of morality, and thereby encouraging their development as moral agents.

The most difficult questions, however, still lie ahead. Even if we have succeeded in showing that we can teach children *about morality*, in the sense that we can convey to them some of the facts and rules associated with it (teaching that...), and some of the skills and procedures it demands (teaching how...), this is far from being the whole story. We

may be able to teach children some of the information and
skills that moral agents need, but can we ensure that they
will *use* that information and *apply* those skills? Can we
teach children not only *about morality*, but also *to be moral*
and *to become moral agents*? It is to this knotty problem that
we must now turn.

6.4 *Teaching to* . . .

Mention was made in Chapter 1 of how teaching children *to*
do X is tied directly to the behaviour (X) which is thereby
learned, in a way in which teaching *that* X is the case, or
teaching *how* to do X, are not. One can teach children a mass
of information, without teaching them *to* use that information; and one can teach them how to do all sorts of things,
without teaching them *to* do those things on appropriate
occasions. These possibilities must be borne in mind when
any form of moral education is attempted, if we are not to
deceive ourselves about what has actually been taught and
learned, for we saw at the end of the previous section that
children may be taught a great deal about morality without
being taught to be moral agents; they may fail to *use* the
information and the skills they have acquired, when faced
with a real-life moral decision, or they may fail to *act* upon
the moral judgements they have formed. Teaching to . . .
must, therefore, play at least as important a part in moral
education as teaching that . . . and teaching how . . .

If this distinction between the different forms of moral
teaching is ignored, the result is often considerable
confusion about the aims of moral education and its
effectiveness. In the United States and Canada, for example,
several moral education programmes have been based upon
Kohlberg's research into moral development, but Kohlberg
is predominantly (though not entirely) concerned with
moral *judgement* and *reasoning*, and has comparatively
little to say about the factors which affect whether or not
children *act* in accordance with their judgements; so, even if
these teaching programmes succeeded in raising children's
levels of moral reasoning, they would not necessarily be
producing moral *agents*. Similarly, in this country the

Schools Council Moral Education Project offers a perfect illustration of the false conclusions which can be drawn, if the necessary distinctions are not heeded. After trying out a unit of its 'Lifeline' material on 300 children, the project found that they had shown 'a 50 per cent increase in the number of points relevant to others' needs, interests and feelings in ten situations *which they recorded in a written test...*' (McPhail, Ungoed-Thomas and Chapman 1972, p.104, my italics). Giving the 'right' answers in a written test (as a result of teaching that... and teaching how...) cannot, of course, indicate that the children have been successfully taught *to* act morally, yet the project immediately concludes: 'Without doubt work of this kind can produce improvements *in behaviour* as well as in attitude...' (my italics).

Can we, then, teach children to act as moral agents? The crucial factor here is not knowledge of facts or procedures, but motivation. When we fail to act as moral agents, though possessing all the required information and skills, it is usually because we do not *want* so to act. It is, unfortunately, a not uncommon human experience to believe that one ought to do something without translating that belief into action, thereby succumbing to the 'gappiness' which Cooper describes as an essential feature of the moral life. Such behaviour is commonly attributed to our 'weakness of will' – a mysterious phenomenon which has fascinated philosophers since the time of Socrates (see Mortimore 1971; Straughan 1982). The most straightforward interpretation, however, of this 'weakness' is that we sometimes simply do not want to do what we believe we ought to do. A girl may, for example, accept that there are good reasons why she *ought* to get home by the time she promised, and to prevent her parents worrying about her safety, but also be influenced by other kinds of reason, which motivate her to *want* to stay out with her friends, with whom she is having a good time.

Teaching children to be moral, then, must become a matter of teaching them to *want* to be moral. The knowledge and abilities which can result from teaching that... and teaching how... are not enough in themselves to ensure this motivation, though it will no doubt often be the case that children *will* want to make use of what they have learned, in forming moral decisions and acting upon them. Clearly, no teaching method can *guarantee* to produce the appropriate motivation and subsequent behaviour, for teaching (unlike conditioning and indoctrination) implies that the learner is a free agent, capable of accepting or rejecting what is taught; and furthermore, the necessary 'gappiness' of morality means that there must always remain the possibility of a moral decision *not* being acted upon.

Nevertheless, if moral education is not to remain a wholly 'theoretical' enterprise, it cannot shut its eyes to the problems of teaching to ... Such teaching cannot consist simply of the transmission of knowledge and skills, so what is it to focus upon? The answer must lie in one of the components of morality which has come to our notice regularly in the earlier chapters, and which now calls for a more systematic analysis – the 'feeling' element.

6.5   Feeling and motivation

When we *want* to do something, we feel attracted or positively inclined towards that action, because we see it or its likely consequences as desirable in some way or other. If our aim is for children to want to be moral, then, we must present moral behaviour to them in as desirable a light as possible, in order that they may feel motivated to act morally. The 'feeling' component of morality and of moral education is, therefore, of enormous practical importance, though it is also the one most open to misinterpretation and distortion. We have already seen, for example, how Hare's account is unsatisfactory in this respect, and how emotivism mistakenly maintains that our moral judgements are *caused* by our feelings, thereby turning moral education (by implication) into a process of emotional manipulation.

The moral function of feeling and emotion, then, and their links with moral motivation need careful examination, for the picture which has emerged so far is an intricate one, which certainly does not portray morality as being 'just a matter of feeling'. We feel that we want to act morally because we *see* a situation in a particular light, which in turn motivates us to do something about it; I may feel that I want to send some money to a famine relief project, for example, because I see this action and portray it to myself as helping to relieve human suffering (which attracts me as a desirable goal) rather than as depleting my bank balance (which is a less motivating prospect). Our judgements and interpretations of situations thus help to determine how we feel about them, which means that moral education cannot start by directly seeking to influence children's feelings and emotions. The area of judgement and understanding cannot be by-passed in this way – not without resorting to drugs, hypnotism and brain surgery, at any rate.

Those concerned with moral education, therefore, need to arrive at a balanced view of the all-important role played by feelings in moral behaviour. Little will be achieved, for instance, by an approach which merely encourages children to 'express their emotions', in the hope that it will aid their moral development, for moral agents often have to *control* their feelings to enable decisions to be made in the cool rather than the heat of the moment. Likewise, although consideration for others (or what Hare calls 'love') represents one obvious goal of moral education, this is not necessarily best fostered by encouraging children to develop feelings of intense affection or loyalty for particular individuals, such as parents, teachers, or friends of either sex, as this might well militate against the 'impersonal' requirements of moral reasoning in situations where the conflicting interests of various people have to be weighed *impartially*.

So what can be done to teach children to want to be moral, bearing in mind these general points about moral feeling and moral motivation? Much will depend upon the age and maturity of the child, for Kohlberg has shown that children are motivated by different considerations at different stages of development. At the lower stages, rewards and punishments loom large as moral incentives and sanctions, and given these 'brute facts of child development', as Peters calls them, it is difficult to see how moral education can begin to exercise any motivational effect without the use of these methods, which have tended to feature prominently in the more traditional forms of 'value transmission', as described in Chapter 2 (2.1). Rewards and punishments serve to tilt the motivational scales, by directly adding to the attractiveness or unattractiveness of the behaviour in question, and therein lie their major strength and weakness. Their strength is that they may succeed in modifying the child's view of a situation, with the result that he comes to want to do that which he sees as reasonable, but which he might otherwise *not* want to do (for example, if Johnny knows that he will be rewarded for looking after his little sister, but punished if he abandons her in the park and goes off to play with his friends instead). The danger of rewards and punishments, on the other hand, is that the child may adopt the habit of acting simply because of the associated incentives and sanctions, and not because he appreciates any moral features of his action; his reasoning may remain at the (non-moral) level of 'What am I going to get out of doing that?' External incentives and sanctions, then, are best seen as a *pre-moral* technique, directed towards controlling and modifying children's motivations and their resultant behaviour, but unlikely to improve their grasp of *moral* reasons, or their willingness to act upon them as such.

What is being taught by rewarding and punishing children is not morality itself, but one facet of morality – consistency. Moral agents have to be consistent in following the rules of moral reasoning, and in translating their conclusions into action. Young children will not, of course, be able to display this degree of maturity and moral consistency, but they can at least start to form the habit of adhering reasonably consistently to certain 'basic rules', partly because of the incentives and sanctions attached to them. This need not be an unacceptably authoritarian process, for to borrow Peters's metaphor it is surely possible to give young children glimpses of the palace of Reason while they are still finding their way around the courtyard of Habit. A parent may, for example, reward Johnny for looking after his little sister, thereby helping to establish the habit of caring for the weak, while at the same time *explaining the reasons* for the reward.

The use of rewards and punishments supported by reasoned explanations, therefore, to teach children to adopt habits of consistent, rule-following behaviour will be particularly appropriate at the earlier stages of moral development, when children are most impressed by such sanctions, and when the 'basic rules' of social living have to be transmitted. But can anything be done to encourage older children to use their increasing knowledge and ability to form moral judgements which they *care* about sufficiently to want to act upon them? Again, no teaching can guarantee such a result, but this does not mean that moral education need be entirely powerless in this respect.

First, there is a sense in which older children can be taught to care about morality in a similar way to that in which they can be taught to care about any other subject which they learn about. A skilled and enthusiastic teacher of, say, history, or science, or mathematics, or language, can convey the flavour of his subject by teaching its distinctive rules and procedures in such a way that some children will come to feel motivated to submit to this particular discipline, to adopt its patterns of reasoning and to solve problems by applying its methods correctly. A major factor in achieving this kind of disciplined commitment will be the personal example set by the teacher, in terms of the satisfaction which he shows can be derived from mastering the subject's procedures and 'getting them right'. It should also be possible for both teachers and parents to convey the flavour of *morality* likewise, by exemplifying the challenge and satisfaction of coming to a rational, justifiable decision about a difficult moral problem. Such solutions cannot, of course, be 'right' in the sense that mathematical solutions can be, but children can still be taught that there are better or worse, satisfactory or unsatisfactory methods of making moral decisions, and so come to *care* about the quality of their moral reasoning.

Secondly, there is the task of teaching children of all ages to interpret situations in moral terms, and to apply moral concepts correctly. Moral terms carry with them overtones of approval and disapproval, which we pick up as young children when we start to encounter moral language. 'That's stealing!' or 'That's cheating!' are not merely descriptive statements; they also express disapproval of the action in question. The moral vocabulary of children reflects this strong 'feeling' element, with the result that a child who has acquired the concept of stealing, or cheating, or cruelty, or unfairness, or laziness, or dishonesty, or greediness, will be disposed to have negative feelings towards behaviour which he classifies as an instance of any of these things; he will not, other things being equal, approve of cruelty and unfairness, and he will not want to be cruel or unfair himself. But how is he to recognize the instances? A child may feel opposed to the idea of 'stealing', yet not classify the action of entering an orchard to pick apples without the owner's permission *as* 'stealing'. What will be most helpful here will be the maximum amount of discussion about how concrete situations can be described and categorized, and how moral concepts can be applied to them – from the level of the 3-year-old, learning that eating more than you want so that others get less is an example of 'greediness', to that of the teenager who realizes that there is a problem over whether the term 'murder' should be applied to abortion, euthanasia, contraception and warfare.

Finally and more specifically, moral education may be able to affect how children feel towards other people, which will in turn affect how they behave towards them. As we have seen that morality is typically (though not exclusively) concerned with interpersonal transactions and relationships, this aspect of moral feeling, and the possibilities of it being 'taught', deserve special consideration and a separate section.

6.6 Feeling for others

A child may accept that there are good, moral reasons why he ought to give up his seat in the bus to an old lady, but if he positively dislikes old ladies in general, or this old lady in particular, he will be less likely to feel moved to want to act as he thinks he ought. The main motivational requirements in this area of morality are a concern for the interests of other people and a desire to promote their welfare. So what forms of moral education might make an effective contribution here?

A variety of *social experience* will be a necessity. The child who dislikes old ladies may have a very limited understanding of them, which could be improved by getting to know more about them. Closer and more regular contact with any group of people will not necessarily, of course, increase one's *liking* for them (our seat-hogging child *might* conclude from his wider experience of old ladies that they are even more cantankerous and ungrateful than he originally thought), but greater knowledge and understanding will often produce greater tolerance, as one becomes more aware of other people's attitudes and beliefs, their hopes and their fears; there will also be less danger of a group being indiscriminately labelled or stereotyped (e.g. as 'old ladies') without due recognition of the individual's uniqueness.

Children cannot, then, learn to consider other people's interests and feelings without knowing quite a lot about how other people live and how they view the world. The scope for moral education here is vast; it could, for example, include many formal and informal school activities, such as producing a play or concert, running a club, taking part in school camps, expeditions, overseas trips and exchange visits, helping to organize fund-raising ventures, and taking part in community projects designed to help the elderly, the sick and the disabled. The programme of activities would naturally have to take account of the children's age and maturity, but the experience of working with others towards a common goal, and at the same time increasing one's understanding of individuals and groups whose interests and viewpoints have previously appeared remote and unimportant, is likely to have a considerable effect on most children's motivational attitudes towards other people.

This kind of social experience will not often feature as a formal part of the school curriculum, and indeed can be encouraged as well by parents, youth leaders and others as by teachers. The school, however, might reasonably be expected to make a distinctive contribution in this crucial area of children's 'feeling for others', and whether or not it decides to offer a specific 'moral education' programme (an issue which will be further discussed in the final section), some of the more traditional elements of the curriculum are worth examining in this connection. We noted in Chapter 2 in connection with the 'values across the curriculum' approach

(2.6) that teachers of literature, for instance, can hardly avoid discussing with their pupils the personalities of fictional characters, and how these affect their ways of thinking and behaving; history can provide similar opportunities to analyse motives and intentions, and thereby increase children's understanding of human behaviour and their powers of empathy, while geography and social studies can illustrate a wide variety of different lifestyles and perspectives, so enlarging the child's concept of a 'person'.

Rather more controversial is the question of what religious education can and should do in this respect. The whole status of religious education on the school curriculum raises many problems which cannot be explored at length here, but what seems particularly relevant to our present investigation is the undeniable fact that religious beliefs are capable of exerting a powerful influence upon how one *feels* and *behaves* towards other people, not simply because of the divine sanctions which may motivate some believers, but also because of the distinctive view that a religion may convey of *what man is*. This is not to grant that it is the school's job to see that 'faith is established', as the Plowden Report surprisingly advocated (1967, para. 572) – an objective bristling with educational, theological and moral difficulties (see Hirst 1965). Nor, of course, is it to accept that children should be taught a particular moral code just because it is prescribed (or thought to be prescribed) by a particular religious authority. Yet to try to avoid these pitfalls by swinging to the opposite extreme, and depriving children of all access to religious interpretations of human experience, is equally unjustifiable, because these interpretations have been and still are instrumental in shaping man's view of the world and of his place in it, including his relations with his fellow men. The validity of this religious perspective certainly cannot be 'proved' like that of a mathematical theorem, but nor can it be similarly 'disproved' – which makes its status not unlike that of other highly respectable curriculum areas, such as art or music or literature (see Straughan 1974).

These points support much of the current thinking about religious education, which sees the aim of the subject to be not 'establishing faith', but rather exploring the nature of religion, in terms of its various beliefs, practices and interpretations (see e.g. Sealey 1985). Conceived of in this way, religious education might help to develop children's concern for others by offering a wide range of alternative 'views of man' for older children to consider and discuss. Although we saw in Chapter 5 that 'facts' about human nature cannot directly supply us with moral rules and principles, there must still be some interconnections between what we think man *is*, what we think is *good* for man and how we think we ought to *treat* other people. If I see other people as my 'brothers', or as soul-possessing 'children of God', my feelings and behaviour towards them are likely to be different from what they would be if I saw man purely as the ultimate evolutionary product of natural selection, or consisting of merely 'four buckets of water and a bagful of salts', as the materialist claims. It is essential to be clear about what 'view of man' we believe to be the most adequate and coherent, for as moral agents we cannot avoid basing our decisions about how to behave towards others partly upon our most fundamental beliefs and assumptions about the *nature* of human beings (see White 1973, pp. 48–9).

The 'views of man' which religious education can bring to children's attention need not and should not all be 'religious' ones, which take for granted the existence of a personal God. The Christian conception of man (or rather the various versions of it) can be discussed alongside the interpretations of other world religions and of non-religious belief systems and doctrines. The Marxist, the Freudian psychoanalyst and the Darwinian biologist, for example, each represents a distinctive viewpoint, while different 'views of man' are also implied in theories of racial supremacy, ecological conservation and 'alternative' technology. All such perspectives contain 'metaphysical' elements in the form of various assumptions about the nature, function and destiny of man, which go beyond mere facts about human beings that we can establish empirically. These assumptions and the values implicit in them can and should be examined carefully with adolescents, in order that they may arrive at their own 'view of man' in as informed and critical a way as possible. A start can also be made with younger children by discussing, for example, the similarities and differences which exist between man and the rest of the animal kingdom.

But should *one* 'view of man' be taught as 'better' or 'more correct' than the others? If children's feelings, attitudes and behaviour are going to be influenced by the interpretation which they accept, should teachers and parents try to promote the interpretation which they believe in, or allow children to make their own choice, free from adult pressure? This question highlights the final problem to which we must now attend.

6.7 Description, evaluation and neutrality

One crucial question has been left in abeyance since it was initially raised in Chapter 3. If there are two senses of 'moral' (the 'descriptive' and the 'evaluative'), and correspondingly two senses of 'moral education', which of these senses should we have in mind when deciding what 'moral' teaching to present to children? Enough has already been said about the descriptive interpretation of moral education to show that a strong case can be made for deliberately and systematically introducing children to the main features of morality's form and content, in order that they may learn to operate within that area as moral agents. Moral questions will confront young people in their everyday lives at least as frequently as, say, scientific or historical or artistic questions, yet the educational effort devoted to improving the standard of moral understanding often seems disproportionate to that expended on the teaching of other forms of understanding. Furthermore, the intricate problems which we have encountered in trying to clarify the nature of morality indicate that moral education needs just as much skilled teaching as any other area of the curriculum, and thus cannot simply be 'left to the parents', any more than can children's scientific or artistic education – though obviously parents can support and supplement the teaching their children receive about morality, just as they can with any other subject, *provided* that their own knowledge and understanding are adequate.

What we have learned from this investigation, therefore, strongly suggests that a descriptive form of moral education at least should be taught in all schools, by teachers who are aware of the complexity of the subject and of the issues it raises. But what about *evaluative* moral education? Is it enough for children just to be taught how morality works, and how moral agents reason and behave? Perhaps teachers and parents should also put forward positive moral views, ideals and codes of behaviour of which they approve, with the intention of getting children to approve of them as well. Or will this more 'committed' approach inevitably be aiming merely at obedience, or conformity, or emotional reactions, none of which has much to do with morality? If these dangers are to be avoided, is a position of strict *neutrality* the only one which the moral educator can legitimately adopt?

Much has been written and spoken in recent years about whether 'neutral teaching' is desirable or even possible, and mention has already been made in this chapter and in Chapter 2 (2.2) of the Humanities Curriculum Project, which was largely responsible for initiating the lively debate on this subject (see Taylor 1975, Section 2; Brown 1975, Pt 4). Rather than attempt a comprehensive summary of this debate, however, it will at this stage be more useful to list briefly a number of points which relate both to the specific problem of evaluative moral education, and also to the general account of morality presented in the earlier chapters. This will serve to underline some of the major issues in the neutrality debate, and at the same time to offer a resolution of our problem about whether we should teach children to be (evaluatively) 'good' as well as (descriptively) 'moral'.

(a) First it must be noted that the distinction between the descriptive and evaluative senses of 'moral' and 'moral education' can become just as blurred as that between the form and content of morality. If I believe that morality is to be *defined* in terms of a particular form of reasoning (for instance, involving universal, prescriptive judgements), or alternatively in terms of a particular set of rules and principles (for instance, concerning fairness and considerateness), then in my role as a moral agent I am going to *approve* of that form of reasoning, or those rules and principles; I shall try to adopt or implement them myself, and be in favour of other people doing likewise. Equally, if my role is that of a moral *educator*, I must logically be in favour of that form of reasoning or those rules and principles being *taught*, because that is what I see morality to be about. So although it is helpful for the purposes of analysis to distinguish in principle between the two senses, in practice they will tend to coalesce as soon as the moral agent or the moral educator comes to form particular judgements and make actual decisions.

The idea of a purely descriptive form of moral education, then, is somewhat unrealistic. Any programme of moral education has to select a certain range of subject matter to be taught, and thereby must denote approval of what is selected as being *relevant* to the child's moral development; such approval is expressed, for example, in deciding that the ability to put oneself in another person's position is morally important, and should therefore form one of the programme's objectives, whereas the ability to pick winners or to pick pockets does not come into this category. Simply to teach children *about* one's conception of morality, without expressing any commitment or favourable attitude towards that conception, would be a very odd enterprise from both the theoretical and the practical points of view. It would certainly give children little idea of what it means to be a moral agent, for the teacher could not be behaving as one himself if he showed no inclination to promote that which he considered to be the main concern of morality.

(b) Need we lament the fact that it appears impracticable to restrict moral education to wholly descriptive teaching? Perhaps there is some positive educational *merit* to be gained from advocating a particular moral point of view to children. Peters's 'paradox of moral education' implies that an evaluative approach of this kind is necessary in the case of young children, but could it not also be justified at other stages? We noted in Chapter 2 that a compelling argument to

this effect is developed by Mary Warnock in her contribution to the neutrality debate, when she claims that the teacher must be a *leader* in argument if he is to teach argument, and must, therefore, *demonstrate* to children how moral arguments are conducted and moral conclusions drawn (2.2). This view is very much in line with what has already been said about learning to be a moral agent, and the importance of demonstration and example. After all, we do not expect a science teacher to maintain his 'neutrality' by refusing to show pupils how scientists actually tackle a scientific problem, or how they draw conclusions from scientific evidence, and a similar point could be made about the teaching of other subjects. Why, then, should the moral educator be shackled in this way?

(c) Granted that it is vital for children's moral education that they see adult moral agents at work, it becomes even more imperative that the examples they witness really *are* of moral agents, and not merely of adults in authority expressing their feelings and preferences. We can now appreciate that there is much more to the business of being a moral agent than merely exhibiting approval or dis- approval, and trying to get others to share one's feelings. Evaluative moral education, then, if it is really to *be* moral education, cannot use any method it likes of transmitting values to the young. *Rational justification* is central to morality, and it is this demanding requirement which can bridge the gap between descriptive and evaluative moral education, so preventing the latter from degenerating into a process of authoritarian imposition or emotional manipulation.

The moral agent seeks to justify his decisions by appealing to reasons and principles which can be rationally discussed, supported and criticized; it is only when he believes his decision to be justified in accordance with morality's procedures that he concludes that that decision is morally right, and so *ought* to be acted upon. Teachers and parents must therefore try to convey that it is the process of rational justification alone which entitles and indeed requires the moral agent to declare his beliefs and commitments.

(d) An evaluative form of moral education, then, which pays due regard to the rational procedures of moral argument, is a necessary and desirable complement to the descriptive form. The very nature of morality, however, makes such positive teaching a delicate and difficult business. On the one hand, Mary Warnock's comments emphasize the need for the teacher or parent to 'clearly express his moral views' and to argue for their superiority over other views; yet on the other hand, we have seen that moral conclusions cannot be proved empirically to be right or wrong, and that moral arguments can always be challenged by bringing forward alternative interpretations of situations and of what is good for man.

How is the moral educator to reconcile these two apparently conflicting features of the 'subject' he is trying to teach? The only reasonable procedure is to acknowledge both: first, by teaching (on some occasions at least) what he himself believes to be morally right or wrong, and *why* he so believes, thus exemplifying what it means to seek to justify a moral viewpoint; and secondly, by *encouraging* critical questioning and appraisal of that viewpoint, so demonstrating the value that he, as a moral agent, places upon independent judgement and rational discussion. By adopting this approach the moral educator is not debarred from declaring and arguing for his own moral beliefs, but he must also strive to convey that all moral conclusions are *provisional*, in the sense that they must be held open to the reasoned criticism of others, however firmly one believes in their validity.

(e) Finally, who is this 'moral educator' to be, and in what context can he best combine his descriptive and evaluative roles? Plenty of hints have already been dropped in this connection, but an explicit answer is now called for. Clearly, intelligent teaching is needed here, and intelligent teaching is to be looked for and (one hopes) found in schools. Moral education, then, must be one of the school's responsibilities, but many would argue that the home has an even more influential part to play. Certainly parents have many opportunities to further their children's moral develop-

ment, but the danger is that they may not have thought hard enough about what they are trying to teach; it is only too easy for the 'moral influence' of the home to finish up having little to do with morality itself, but a lot to do with domestic convenience, socialization and the mere imposition of parental authority. If parents are to claim the title of moral educators, they must learn to do more than just declare their own opinions in the hope that their children will conform to them.

A similar point can be made about the school's responsibility for moral education. As was mentioned in Chapter 2 (2.1), there is currently so much airy talk about the 'hidden curriculum' and 'value transmission' that many teachers seem to assume that enough moral education is going on anyway in schools, without extra teaching time being set aside for it. This is a confused assumption, however, for there may be all the difference in the world between 'value transmission' and moral education. No doubt many of children's attitudes and values are shaped and modified by such 'hidden' factors as the way a school is organized, the language that teachers use, the clothes they wear, the things they smile at and the things they frown at, but to be influenced unconsciously in this manner is not to be morally educated. Indeed, it may be a necessary part of moral education to make children more aware of the 'values' which are being thus 'transmitted', in order that they may examine them openly and critically, rather than assimilate them unthinkingly.

Equally misleading is the claim that all teachers are already 'doing moral education' through the medium of other subjects, and that no further provision is consequently needed. It is true that a moral dimension can be introduced into the teaching of most subjects, as was illustrated in the case of literature, history, social studies, science and religious education (2.6), but not all teachers avail themselves of such opportunities, and even when they do there is no guarantee that they will have the same understanding of morality as they have of their specialist subject. Considering the complex nature of the moral area, it seems presumptuous for a teacher of English or history or biology to believe that he can happily deal 'off the cuff' with any moral issues which impinge upon his subject, when he would probably be unwilling to let a 'non-specialist' loose upon his own area of teaching.

There must always be a risk, therefore, that any unsystematic or unplanned attempt at moral education, particularly in the evaluative sense, will turn out to be unrelated to either morality or education. Rigorous thinking about the 'typical features' of morality and the best means of teaching these to children is essential, if we are to avoid the many unexamined and inadequate interpretations of moral education that have come to our notice throughout this book.

This final chapter, while not trying to formulate a detailed teaching handbook for moral education, has shown how a variety of practical implications for teaching in this area can be derived from an analysis of what it means to be morally good. Our conclusion is that moral education, of both a descriptive and an evaluative kind, can and should be tackled in a number of different ways, in at least three different contexts – by parents in the home, by all teachers in their everyday teaching, and by 'specialist' teachers in planned 'moral' programmes of lessons and activities. Even this concentrated effort cannot *ensure* that children will be taught to be good, for morally educating a child cannot be as mechanical a process as house-training a puppy, but the approaches which have been described in this chapter, and implied in the earlier ones, should at least give young people every opportunity to become participant members of the moral community.

Further Reading

The main aim of this book has been to illustrate the inter-connections between moral philosophy and moral education, and to show how questions about the latter cannot be satisfactorily tackled without some acquaintance with the former. If the reader has grasped this vital point, and in doing so has increased his or her understanding of *some* of the problem areas in both moral philosophy and moral education, the book will have achieved its central objective, but it must be emphasized that it has not attempted what would be impossible (given that this is intended as a relatively brief, introductory text) – namely, to present a comprehensive analysis of all aspects of moral philosophy, or of all the philosophical issues raised by moral education.

If the reader wishes to investigate these matters further, many of the references given in the text will provide useful starting-points. These have, however, been kept to a minimum, as it would be easy for a book of this kind to end up consisting of more references than text; also, the flow of what has been (one hopes) a developing and coherent argument would have been fatally disrupted, if every page were littered with cross-references, documenting all the points of support, opposition and qualification which could be quoted.

In addition to the textual references, therefore, some additional guidance for further reading may be helpful. As we have been looking at two distinct, though related, areas (those of moral philosophy and moral education), each with its own extensive literature, it will be most convenient to treat these separately in making the following suggestions, which are based mainly on grounds of readability, accessibility and relevance to the issues highlighted in this book.

(1) Moral Philosophy

There are a number of good introductions to moral philosophy as a whole, which demonstrate that the range of the subject extends far beyond the topics discussed in this book. The following can be particularly recommended for their clarity of presentation:

Raphael, D.D., *Moral Philosophy* (Oxford: OUP, 1981).
Hospers, J., *Human Conduct* (New York: Harcourt Brace Jovanovich, 1972).
Warnock, G.J., *Contemporary Moral Philosophy* (London: Macmillan, 1967).
Warnock, M., *Ethics since 1900* (Oxford: OUP, 1960).
Ewing, A.C., *Ethics* (London: English Universities Press, 1953).
Hudson, W.D., *Modern Moral Philosophy* (London: Macmillan, 1970).
MacIntyre, A.C., *A Short History of Ethics* (London: Routledge & Kegan Paul, 1967).
Williams, B., *Morality* (Cambridge: CUP, 1972). *Ethics and the Limits of Philosophy* (London: Fontana, 1985).
Mackie, J.L., *Ethics: Inventing Right and Wrong* (Harmondsworth: Penguin, 1977).
Trusted, J., *Moral Principles and Social Values* (London: Routledge & Kegan Paul, 1987).

More succinct summaries and critiques of various ethical theories are offered by several philosophers of education, notably:

Peters, R.S., *Ethics and Education* (London: Allen & Unwin, 1966), ch. 3.
Hirst, P.H., *Moral Education in a Secular Society* (London: University of London Press, 1974), ch. 3.
Barrow, R., *Moral Philosophy for Education* (London: Allen & Unwin, 1975), ch. 2.

(2) Moral Education

Psychologists and sociologists, as well as philosophers, are interested in moral education, and a number of references have been made in this book to empirical work such as Piaget's and Kohlberg's, of which philosophers have to take some account. This point is well illustrated in a book which was one of the first to stimulate the current interest and research in moral education, and which remains one of the best introductions to the subject: J.

Wilson, N. Williams and B. Sugarman, *Introduction to Moral Education* (Harmondsworth: Penguin, 1967). A more recent attempt at a simple, overall survey of the subject is: M. Downey and A.V. Kelly, *Moral Education, Theory and Practice* (London: Harper & Row, 1978).

The philosophical aspects of moral education have in themselves, however, generated a formidable amount of writing, from which the following highly selective reading list has been compiled. The work of John Wilson and of Richard Peters has been particularly influential, and for this reason a selection of their work is given first.

J. Wilson, N. Williams and B. Sugarman, *Introduction to Moral Education* (Harmondsworth: Penguin, 1967) – Wilson's own philosophical section is in Part 1. Many of the ideas here are developed and elaborated in his later books and articles, notably:
Education in Religion and the Emotions (London: Heinemann, 1971).
The Assessment of Morality (Windsor, Berks: NFER, 1973).
A Teacher's Guide to Moral Education (London: Geoffrey Chapman, 1973).
Practical Problems in Moral Education (London: Heinemann, 1973).
Discipline and Moral Education (Windsor, Berks: NFER/ Nelson, 1981).

Most of Peters's major work on moral education is to be found in his *Psychology and Ethical Development* (London: Allen & Unwin, 1974), especially Part Two, in *Moral Development and Moral Education* (London: Allen & Unwin, 1981) and in *Reason and Compassion* (London: Routledge & Kegan Paul, 1973). These contain articles on the theories of Freud, Piaget and Kohlberg, and on many aspects of children's moral development.

Other books which may be found particularly helpful are:

Taylor, M. (ed.), *Progress and Problems in Moral Education* (Windsor, Berks: NFER, 1975).
Chazan, B.I., and Soltis, J.F. (eds), *Moral Education* (Columbia, NY: Teachers College Press, 1975).
Hirst, P.H., *Moral Education in a Secular Society* (London: University of London Press, 1974).
Sizer, T., and N. (eds), *Moral Education: Five Lectures* (Cambridge, Mass.: Harvard University Press, 1970).

Crittenden, B., *Form and Content in Moral Education* (Toronto: Ontario Institute for Studies in Education, 1972).

Rowson, R., *Moral Education* (Milton Keynes: Open University Press, 1973).

Straughan, R., *I Ought To, But . . .: A Philosophical Approach to the Problem of Weakness of Will in Education* (Windsor, Berks: NFER/Nelson, 1982).

Brown, S.C., (ed.), *Philosophers Discuss Education* (London: Macmillan, 1975) – Part Four.

Elliott, J., and Pring, R. (eds), *Social Education and Social Understanding* (London: University of London Press, 1975).

Bridges, D., and Scrimshaw, P., *Values and Authority in Schools* (London: Hodder & Stoughton, 1975).

Hersh, R.H., Miller, J.P. and Fielding, G.D., *Models of Moral Education* (New York: Longman, 1980).

Pring, R., *Personal and Social Education in the Curriculum* (London: Hodder & Stoughton, 1984).

Thacker, J., Pring, R., and Evans, D. (eds.), *Personal, Social and Moral Education in a Changing World* (Windsor, Berks: NFER/Nelson, 1987).

Weinreich-Haste, H., and Locke, D. (eds.), *Morality in the Making* (Chichester: Wiley, 1983) – especially Section II.

Carter, R.E., *Dimensions of Moral Education* (Toronto: University of Toronto Press, 1984).

Ward, L.O., (ed.), *The Ethical Dimension of the School Curriculum* (Swansea: Pineridge, 1982).

Spiecker, B. and Straughan, R. (eds.) *Philosophical Issues in Moral Education and Development* (Milton Keynes: Open University Press, 1988).

Articles on all aspects of moral education also frequently appear in educational journals. Those written from a philosophical perspective are most likely to be found in the *Journal of Moral Education* and the *Journal of Philosophy of Education*.

References

Aristotle, *Ethics*, trans. J.A.K. Thompson (Harmondsworth: Penguin, 1955).

Ayer, A.J., *Language, Truth and Logic* (London: Gollancz, 1936).

Baier, K., 'Moral autonomy as an aim of moral education', in *New Essays in the Philosophy of Education*, eds G. Langford and D.J. O'Connor (London: Routledge & Kegan Paul, 1973), pp. 96–114.

Brown, S.C. (ed.), *Philosophers Discuss Education* (London: Macmillan, 1975).

Bullock Report, *A Language for Life* (London: HMSO, 1975).

Butler, J., 'Sermon II upon human nature', in *Butler's Works*, ed. W.E. Gladstone (London: OUP, 1897).

Chazan, B.I., and Soltis, J.F. (eds), *Moral Education* (Columbia, NY: Teachers College Press, 1975).

Cooper, N., 'Oughts and wants' and 'Further thoughts on oughts and wants', in *Weakness of Will*, ed. G.W. Mortimore (London: Macmillan, 1971), pp. 190–9 and 216–25.

DES/HMI, *Aspects of Secondary Education in England* (London: HMSO, 1979).

DES/HMI, *A View of the Curriculum* (London: HMSO, 1980).

Flugel, J.C., *Man, Morals and Society* (London: Duckworth, 1945).

Foot, P., 'Moral beliefs', in *Theories of Ethics*, ed. P. Foot (London: OUP, 1967), pp. 83–100.

Fraenkel, J.P., *How to Teach about Values: an Analytic Approach* (New Jersey: Prentice-Hall, 1977).

Goodall, O., Beale, M., Beleschenko, A. and Murchison, P., *Developing Social Awareness in Young Children* (University of Exeter School of Education: Workbook Series 4, 1983).

Hare, R.M., *The Language of Morals* (London: OUP, 1952).

Hare, R.M., *Freedom and Reason* (London: OUP, 1963).

Hare, R.M., 'Language and moral education', in *New Essays in the Philosophy of Education*, eds. G. Langford and D.J. O'Connor (London: Routledge & Kegan Paul, 1973), pp. 149-66.

Hare, R.M., *Moral Thinking* (London: OUP, 1981).

Hersh, R.H., Miller, J.P. and Fielding, G.D., *Models of Moral Education* (New York: Longman, 1980).

Hirst, P.H., 'Morals, religion and the maintained school', *British Journal of Educational Studies*, vol. 14, 1965, pp. 5-18.

Hirst, P.H., *Moral Education in a Secular Society* (London: University of London Press, 1974).

Hudson, W.D., (ed.), *The Is-Ought Question* (London: Macmillan, 1969).

Kohlberg, L., 'Education for justice: a modern statement of the Platonic view', in *Moral Education: Five Lectures*, eds. T. Sizer and N. Sizer (Cambridge, Mass.: Harvard University Press, 1970), pp. 57-83.

Kohlberg, L., 'Moral stages and moralization', in *Moral Development and Behaviour*, ed. T. Lickona (New York: Holt, Rinehart & Winston, 1976).

Kohlberg, L., 'Revisions in the theory and practice of moral development in *Moral Development*, ed. W. Damon (San Francisco: Jossey Bass, 1978).

Kohlberg, L., *The Psychology of Moral Development* (San Francisco: Harper & Row, 1984).

Kolnai, A., 'Erroneous conscience', *Proceedings of the Aristotelean Society*, vol. LXIII, 1957-8, pp. 171-99.

Locke, D., 'Moral development as the goal of moral education' in *Philosophers on Education*, eds. R. Straughan and J. Wilson (Basingstoke: Macmillan, 1987).

McPhail, P., Ungoed-Thomas, J.R., and Chapman, H., *Moral Education in the Secondary School* (London: Longman, 1972).

Milgram, S., *Obedience to Authority* (London: Tavistock, 1974).

Modgil, S., and Modgil, C., (eds.) *Lawrence Kohlberg: Consensus and Controversy* (Lewes: Falmer Press, 1986).

Moore, G.E., *Principia Ethica* (Cambridge: CUP, 1903).

Mortimore, G.W. (ed.), *Weakness of Will* (London: Macmillan, 1971).

Musgrave, P.W., *The Moral Curriculum: a Sociological Analysis* (London: Methuen, 1978).

Neill, A.S., *Summerhill* (Harmondsworth: Penguin, 1968).

Nowell-Smith, P.H., *Ethics* (Harmondsworth: Penguin, 1954).

Paton, H.J. (ed.), *The Moral Law* (London: Hutchinson, 1948).

Peters, R.S., *Ethics and Education* (London: Allen & Unwin, 1966).

Peters, R.S., *Psychology and Ethical Development* (London: Allen & Unwin, 1974).

Phillips, D.Z., and Mounce, H.O., 'On morality's having a point', in *The Is–Ought Question*, ed. W.D. Hudson (London: Macmillan, 1969), pp. 228–39.

Piaget, J., *The Moral Judgement of the Child* (London: Routledge & Kegan Paul, 1932).

Plowden Committee on Primary Education, *Children and their Primary Schools*, Vol. 1 (London: HMSO, 1967).

Pring, R., 'Personal and Social Education' in *The Ethical Dimension of the School Curriculum*, ed. L.O. Ward (Swansea: Pineridge, 1982).

Purpel, D. and Ryan, K. (eds.) *Moral Education ... it comes with the Territory* (Berkeley: Delta Kappa, 1976).

Raths, L., Harmin, M., and Simon, S., *Values and Teaching* (Columbus, Ohio: Charles E. Merrill, 1966).

Rousseau, J.J., *Emile* (London: Dent, 1961).

Ryle, G., 'Conscience and moral convictions', in his *Collected Papers*, Vol. II (London: Hutchinson, 1971).

Sampson, G., *English for the English* (Cambridge: CUP, 1921).

Sartre, J.P., *Existentialism and Humanism* (London: Eyre Methuen, 1973).

Scheffler, I., *The Language of Education* (Springfield, Ill.: Charles C. Thomas, 1960).

Schools Council Nuffield Humanities Project, *The Humanities Project: An Introduction* (London: Heinemann, 1970).

Sealey, J., *Religious Education: Philosophical Perspectives* (London: Allen & Unwin, 1985).

Shaver, J.P., and Strong, W., *Facing Value Decisions* (New York: Teachers College Press, 1982).

Simon, S., Howe, L., and Kirschenbaum, H., *Values Clarification* (New York; A & W Visual Library, 1972).

Stevenson, C.L., *Ethics and Language* (New Haven, Conn.: Yale University Press, 1944).

Straughan, R., 'Religion, morality and the curriculum', *London Educational Review*, vol. 3, no. 3, 1974, pp. 73–9.

Straughan, R., *I Ought To, But ...: A Philosophical Approach to the Problem of Weakness of Will in Education* (Windsor,

Berks: NFER/Nelson, 1982).

Straughan, R., and Wrigley, J. (eds), *Values and Evaluation in Education* (London: Harper & Row, 1980).

Taylor, M. (ed.), *Progress and Problems in Moral Education* (Windsor, Berks: NFER, 1975).

Thalberg, I., 'Acting against one's better judgement' in *Weakness of Will*, ed. G.W. Mortimore (London: Macmillan, 1971), pp. 233–46.

Warnock, G.J., *Contemporary Moral Philosophy* (London: Macmillan, 1967).

Warnock, M., 'The neutral teacher', in *Philosophers Discuss Education*, ed. S.C. Brown (London: Macmillan, 1975), pp. 159–71.

White, J.P., *Towards a Compulsory Curriculum* (London: Routledge & Kegan Paul, 1973).

Wilson, J., *The Assessment of Morality* (Windsor, Berks: NFER, 1973).

Wilson, J., Williams, N., and Sugarman, B., *Introduction to Moral Education* (Harmondsworth: Penguin, 1967).

Index